EDDIE WOO

Superstar Maths Teacher

Aussie STEM Stars

EDDIE WOO
Superstar Maths Teacher

Story told by REBECCA LIM

WILD DINGO PRESS

Aussie STEM Stars series
Published by Wild Dingo Press
Melbourne, Australia
books@wilddingopress.com.au
wilddingopress.com.au

This work was first published by Wild Dingo Press 2021
Text copyright © Rebecca Lim

The moral right of the author has been asserted.

Reproduction and communication for educational purposes:
The Australian *Copyright Act 1968* (the Act) allows a maximum of
one chapter or 10% of the pages of this work, whichever is the greater, to be
reproduced and/or communicated by an educational institution for its educational
purposes provided that the educational institution (or the body that administers it)
has given a remuneration to Copyright Agency under the Act.
For details of the Copyright Agency licence for educational institutions contact:

Copyright Agency
Level 11, 66 Goulburn Street
Sydney NSW 2000
Email: info@copyright.com.au

Reproduction and communication for other purposes:
Except as permitted under the *Copyright Act 1968*, no part of this book may be
reproduced, stored in a retrieval system, or transmitted in any form or by any
means without prior written permission.
All inquiries should be made to the Publisher, Wild Dingo Press.

Cover Design: Gisela Beer
Illustrations: Diana Silkina
Maths diagrams: Eddie Woo
Series Editor: Catherine Lewis
Printed in Australia

Lim, Rebecca 1972-, author.
Eddie Woo: Superstar Maths Teacher / Rebecca Lim

A catalogue record for this
book is available from the
National Library of Australia

ISBN: 9781925893403 (paperback)
ISBN: 9781925893410 (epdf)
ISBN: 9781925893427 (epub)

*'I only have one rule in my classroom
and I call it the human rule. It's very simple.
I will treat you like a human
and I expect you to treat me like a human, too.'*
— **Eddie Woo**

Disclaimer
This work has been developed in collaboration with Eddie Woo. The utmost care has been taken to respectfully portray, as accurately as memory allows, the events and the stories of all who appear in this work. The publishers assume no liability or responsibility for unintended inaccuracies, but would be pleased to rectify at the earliest opportunity any omissions or errors brought to their notice.

Contents

1. A target for bullies — 1
2. Making sacrifices — 16
3. It's okay to be an outsider — 28
4. Getting stronger all the time — 36
5. 'Maths is not really my thing' — 48
6. The fight of her life — 63
7. A chance encounter — 81
8. Mathematics is a sense — 90
9. Mister Wootube — 104
10. Where empathy gets you — 119
11. Be a mathematician — 128

Eddie's beautiful universe of patterns and connections — 149

Resources — 157

About Rebecca Lim — 158

1

A target for bullies

'What've you got there, slant-eyes?'

Eddie hugged his backpack tightly, mentally kicking himself. Why had he brought his favourite adventure puzzle book to school? He must have read that puzzle book cover to cover at least 400 times. It was one of his most prized possessions.

Eddie stared up at the ring of bigger boys standing around him, his stomach churning with the usual sick feeling he had when he was cornered. No matter how fast Eddie ran, or how hard he tried to catch a teacher's attention, the bullies always found him and hurt him, and no one ever saw anything. One of the bullies today was even from Eddie's own Year 3 class! But when Eddie tried to look him in the eye, the boy looked away quickly. They all knew that what they were doing was wrong – picking on someone just because he looked different to them, who was smaller than they were. But they still did it *every single day*. That was the worst thing.

Eddie couldn't change the fact that he was Chinese or skinny or short for his age, that he had serious asthma, and eczema so bad that his face was usually swollen and puffy and he often scratched until his skin bled. He couldn't help that he was born so allergic to dust that he was always sneezing, sniffing and blowing his nose. The old books and carpet at school, even the carpet at home which his parents didn't have the money to replace, often made Eddie really sick, and his mum, Angela, did at least one full load of laundry a day to try to keep Eddie's allergies under control. Eddie was always covered in Band-Aids and Vaseline. He couldn't change the way he looked, or the fact that he loved to read and think and do puzzles. He couldn't change any of the things that were a part of him and made him who he was. But the bullies still hated Eddie just for being himself. And since his protective older sister, Kylie – who used to look out for him in the playground – had gone to high school last year, the bullying had only got worse. While he was at school, it felt like he really had no one in his corner.

Eddie had known what was waiting for him that day at school – more shoving and tripping, punching and kicking, chasing and name-calling. He'd told his mum that something just like this would happen but she'd said, 'You have to go to school today, *Boh*. You have to try. Please? For me.' Eddie's mum always called him *Boh*, which means 'treasure' in Cantonese.

He'd wanted to stay in bed this morning. He'd tried so hard to pretend he was asleep long after the time he knew he was supposed to be up, dressed and at the breakfast table, eating. But his mum didn't give up on him getting to school today, and now here he was, in the firing line again. He'd packed his favourite puzzle book without thinking, just to help him survive lunchtime and recess on his own, hiding out in the school's small, pokey library, or under a tree. Now he hugged his backpack tighter, knowing he'd made a terrible mistake.

Please, not this *puzzle book*, he thought desperately.

Eddie couldn't understand what the bullies wanted, why they kept coming after him or why they never stopped. Almost the hardest part about the bullying was not the physical injuries that Eddie often received – bruises, grazes and cuts – but the feeling that no one, not a single other student or teacher in the entire place, *cared* what happened to him. There were only two other Asian children at Eddie's school, and Eddie often wondered if they copped it like he did. He hoped they didn't. No one should ever have to go through the things that he went through at school. It was the *un*-safest place in Eddie's life.

At that moment, the morning bell rang. Eddie had run to school so late today that the bullies didn't have enough time to land any proper punches or kicks. There was no time left to do that. So all the boys did this morning was bump him with their shoulders so hard as they brushed past, laughing loudly, that Eddie fell over in the dirt, on his face. He landed on top of his backpack and on top of his already dog-eared, precious book. The hard shape of his lunchbox dug painfully into his ribs.

'Catch you later,' one of the boys hissed over his shoulder at where Eddie lay face down on the ground.

'*Drop* you later, you mean!' another one hooted over Eddie's head.

For a long moment, Eddie didn't move, a slow tear trickling down his cheek and hitting the dirt. As usual, none of the teachers had even noticed what had happened and certainly hadn't jumped up to protect him, or to punish the bullies. Eddie reckoned that even if he blew a whistle and waved his arms in the air while standing on tippy-toes or jumping around, no one would see him or pay him the slightest bit of attention.

As Eddie sat up, scrubbing at his face with the back of one hand, he felt *invisible*. He wished he could stay that way forever, but he knew that, before too long, the bullies would find him again.

*

During class, when their form teacher wasn't looking, the boy in Eddie's class who'd stood with the other bullies turned and mouthed things at Eddie like '*You're dead!*' and kept pushing his fingers into the outside corners of his eyes and pulling them up, making horrible faces in Eddie's direction. The other kids in the class nudged each other, whispering and watching to see what would happen, but Eddie never spoke up about it, and no one ever came to help him when things like this occurred. The only real friend Eddie had had since starting primary school had moved away last year.

Not for the first time, Eddie felt completely alone and felt like he didn't matter. He'd never really told his parents about all of the different, awful ways he was being bullied at school because he didn't want to worry them. But he also knew from the stories his parents had told him about how they were treated when they first came to Australia, that being treated badly or being called rude names just came with looking 'different'. It was almost like the price they had to pay for being allowed to live here. Eddie knew that without any real proof of what the bullies were doing to him, his parents wouldn't be able to complain to the school. They might even be told that Eddie was making up stories. Eddie didn't want to get himself and his parents in trouble. It felt like an impossible situation to a kid as small, and as friendless, as Eddie was.

He could barely concentrate on what the teacher was writing on the whiteboard now because he was worrying about his favourite adventure puzzle book. He was flicking through all the dog-eared, familiar pages in his mind – tracing all the pictures and clues and puzzles with his mind's eye – knowing that he would never see them the same way ever again. Not after today. He knew that history was about to repeat itself.

When the bell rang for recess Eddie ran, as he always did at school, straight to his backpack, which was hanging on a hook outside the classroom.

As usual, his bag was already open – but not by him – all the pockets unzipped, with some of his things tipped out and scattered across the floor. Eddie knew exactly who'd done it.

And he knew what he'd find before he even put his hand inside the main compartment.

His lunchbox was gone. He'd expected that. He had no appetite now, anyway.

His Rubik's cube was gone. He'd forgotten that was in there and mentally kicked himself some more.

But worst of all, his favourite adventure puzzle book was gone. He'd known it would happen as soon as he'd set foot within the school boundaries today, but feeling around in the empty space where the book should have been made Eddie's heart thump faster and all the blood rush up into his face.

The bullies had stolen his things again and there was no one he could tell because he couldn't *prove* any of it.

Eddie clenched his fists while around him, the kids on either side pushed and shoved at him to get to their bags, shooting him sideways glances and sly smiles. He wanted to scream, he wanted to howl and punch and kick them the same way people treated him. But he didn't, even though he desperately felt like lashing out and hurting people, the same way he was hurt all the time.

Eddie ran out into the schoolyard, searching desperately. The bullies didn't have much of an imagination and followed the same pattern every time. He found the first piece of his torn puzzle book under the tree where a lot of the kids ate their lunch. He found another ripped piece by the drinking fountain, and another under the monkey bars, and other pieces and pages scattered all across the playground. His favourite puzzle book had just suffered the same fate as all the other puzzle books he'd brought to school to keep him company.

Like always, he was too little and too afraid to tell the teachers what had happened, to show them all the pieces of something he'd loved with all his heart that was now utterly destroyed. And just like always, he went around, silently gathering up every torn-up piece of his book that he could find, in the hope that he might somehow tape it back together when he got home and it would be as good as new. But he never could. His precious puzzle books were always completely ruined – stomped on, ripped, muddied or held under a tap until the pages were a gluey mess – along with his day.

At home that night, in tears, he told his mum, 'I'm *never* going to fit in'.

And his mum told him again that their sacrifices – in coming to Australia and in staying here – would be worth it. 'It's a long game, *Boh*,' his mum told him gently. 'You'll get choices that your Dad and I never had. You just have to stick it out. It *will* get better, I promise you.'

But Eddie didn't understand then, what all that meant. All he knew was that he didn't know how he could stand the bullying any longer. It didn't feel like anything would ever change, or get any better.

To Eddie, school seemed like the kind of endless hell he learnt about on Sundays, at church.

Not for him, *at all*.

*

After his older sister, Kylie, left for high school, from the age of seven onwards, Eddie walked to and from school by himself each day.

He wasn't a very good runner, but as soon as his primary school was in sight he would start running as fast, and as hard, as he could to get past any bullies waiting to rough him up at the gates. At the end of the day, he did the same thing in reverse. But because he was small, and not very fast, and always loaded down with the books he'd borrowed from the library, the bullies would often be waiting to beat him up at whichever gate Eddie tried to leave by. It felt as if they had a scanner set to his particular frequency. Wherever he was, there they'd be. The bullies would throw his things around, leaving Eddie crumpled on the ground, along with his possessions, when they were done.

As Eddie dodged the blows at the gate this morning, the hot summer sun was already beating down and inflaming his already dry, painful and cracked skin. His mum had covered him in Vaseline to try to stop Eddie itching during the course of the long day ahead, but it only made him look puffy and strange and shiny, and the boys laughed in disgust as their hands slid off from around Eddie's neck and arms. They made sure they cleaned their hands all over Eddie's uniform and backpack after they were done.

After lunch spent alone in the stifling hot library away from the bullies, Eddie returned to his Year 3 classroom feeling as if he was on fire, or being bitten by an army of ants, from the intense heat and the scratchiness of his clothes.

'Get your Maths books out!' his teacher ordered. 'Turn to page 32 and do Units 2 and 3. No looking at anyone else's work.'

Maths, ugh, Eddie thought.

Maths was *not* his thing. English and History were. Stories, characters and narratives were where he felt most at home. Those subjects seemed to fire his imagination in a way that Maths *didn't*. Just like he was at school, with Maths, Eddie felt like an *outsider*. Maths made no sense to him the same way that bullying, and having to attend school to *be* bullied, made no sense to him. Eddie would never have dreamt of bullying someone else. So, having people do that to him, day in, day out, just didn't compute at all.

There was a quiet groan throughout the classroom as everyone turned to the right place in their Maths book and started working quietly. Meanwhile, in the suffocating heat of the classroom, the sweat trickled and trickled through Eddie's hair making him scratch his itching head, face and neck. As he worked away at his least favourite subject of all, he scratched and scratched and scratched without thinking about what he was doing. Minute by minute he felt hotter and itchier.

Suddenly, Eddie's teacher raised her head and glared at him, yelling at him loudly from the front of the classroom, 'Eddie Woo! You're deliberately disrupting the rest of the class! Go to the Principal's office right *now*!' Eddie didn't even have time to explain about his burning eczema because she shot to her feet and threw open the classroom door, pointing angrily at the corridor outside.

Stunned and still scratching, Eddie found himself sitting outside the Principal's office in tears. He'd never gotten into trouble for anything in his life ever before. People caused *him* trouble all the time, but no one ever saw it. After that day, Eddie felt an even deeper mistrust of school and his teachers – who never seemed to see what he was going through even though it was happening right under their noses; and especially his classroom teacher, who treated him like a nuisance, not a real person.

For the rest of the year, Eddie felt that he couldn't even scratch or cough or sneeze if his teacher was in the room and it felt like torture when he struggled to stop himself doing that.

Even after he left her class, the sight of this teacher in the playground would cause Eddie to run and hide behind a wall, or under a bench, so that there was no chance she would ever be able to yell at him again, for anything.

Between the teachers who didn't see him and the bullies who looked out for him all the time in order to torment him, Eddie was fast turning into a *school refuser* – someone who would do anything to skip school as much as he could because school made him utterly miserable.

2

Making sacrifices

It didn't seem to matter that Eddie was born in Camperdown, New South Wales, or supported the Parramatta Eels rugby league football club or that his favourite food was fried potato scallops, just like lots of other kids at his school. He just didn't *look* 'Australian' to the bullies at his school even though he was as Australian as they were. Those bullies hated him for lots of reasons, but mostly because he was an ethnic Chinese-Australian kid living in an area of northwest Sydney that didn't have a lot of Chinese or Asian people living in it. The Woo Family stood out in 'The Hills' in those days, and Eddie's older brother and older sister were also called terrible names in the street, and at their school, where kids sang rude songs about Chinese people right to their faces and gave each other 'Chinese burns' without a second thought, thinking it was totally hilarious.

Eddie's dad, Tony, who'd come to Australia in 1969 to finish his last two years of high school and later studied economics at the Australian National University in Canberra, remembered being called horrible names, too. Back when he first came to Australia, a ghastly official policy called the 'White Australia Policy' was only just coming to an end. That policy meant that people who were not 'European' were usually not allowed to come to, or live permanently in, Australia. The policy meant that First Nations people – whose country this was, is and always will be – and non-white or so-called 'coloured' people – especially Asian people – were not welcome here, by law. It also meant that the few Asian people who lived in Australia in the 1970s and 1980s were the targets of constant racism – adults *and* children, whether they were *migrants* (people who'd come to Australia for economic reasons) or *refugees* (people fleeing their home countries because of danger). In some parts of Australia, people threw bricks through the windows of Chinese restaurants or spray-painted racist, hurtful graffiti about Asians everywhere, like, *Stop the Asian Invasion!* And, *Asians out!*

Incidents like these made Eddie's parents really, really sad, but they told Eddie it was an unfortunate fact of life in the 'lucky country'.

'*Boh*, you can't control other people's thoughts, how others feel or the way they treat you,' Eddie's mum would tell him gently. 'The only thing you can control is how you react to things that happen to you. You have to ignore it and move on. Life isn't always going to be fair.'

When Eddie's dad had first come to Australia as a teenager, he reminded Eddie, the people he'd stayed with used to give him less food to eat than they would give themselves, even though he was *paying* them to look after him. He'd had to move house three times in his first year in Australia because he'd had trouble understanding the people he stayed with, and they'd had trouble understanding him, and didn't want him in their homes anymore. It had been really hard and hurtful. Eddie's dad had come to Australia from Kuala Lumpur with three friends from his old school, but they'd all ended up going to a different Australian high school from him.

'So, Eddie,' his dad told him once, when Eddie was refusing to go to school the next day, 'I know exactly what it feels like to be completely alone, without anyone to talk to. And I got through it. You will, too.'

The stories Eddie's dad told him about when he was a high school student in Australia didn't make Eddie feel any better at all. His dad had been treated really badly because he was Chinese and it was still happening now, years and years later – only to Eddie this time.

On more and more days, Eddie refused to go to school when his mum knocked on his bedroom door and said, 'It's time to go now, *Boh*, or you'll be late'.

'I don't want to go!' he would wail in reply from under his doona. 'I don't want to be spoken to like that or be treated like that! I don't want to be beaten up on my way home anymore.'

On the really bad mornings, when something had happened at school the day before that made Eddie feel so sad and angry that he felt hopeless and couldn't get out of bed, his mum never yelled at him or made him feel bad about it. Instead, she would spend time with him, discussing whatever Eddie could bring himself to tell her about what had happened with the bullies the day before, and help him to calm down and feel better. She would tell him about why she and Eddie's dad had come to Australia – to make a better life than they could have had in the country that they came from, Malaysia. Where people who were Chinese, like Eddie's family, weren't allowed to do certain jobs or own certain things or homes or even get places at university, just because they were Chinese, not Malay. Like the 'White Australia Policy' in Australia, there were official government policies in place in Malaysia that made life harder for every person who was not of indigenous Malay descent.

'That's why we came to this land of opportunity, *Boh*,' his mum would remind him gently. 'This is why we're here now and not still living in Malaysia where we have lots and lots of family and friends and a long history. It's worth it, *Boh*, you'll see. But you have to stick through tough times to get to the good parts. It will get better, I promise.'

Eddie would listen to these stories quietly, but it didn't seem like it was any better being Chinese here than it was being Chinese in Malaysia. Being Chinese brought all sorts of pain, for everyone in the Woo family, but especially for him. He wasn't good at making friends like his older brother and sister were. He often felt tongue-tied, or just plain terrified. Eddie wasn't allowed to read his books, eat his lunch or walk home from school in peace, just because he was Chinese, and he hated it.

'School sucks!' Eddie would scream. 'I'm never going back to school ever again!'

When Eddie did that, his mum would distract him with amazing stories about how she'd once been a glamorous newsreader on a TV station in Kuala Lumpur, the capital of Malaysia. It made him forget about the bullies for a while and marvel at this whole other life his mum had had before she'd married his dad and come here, way back

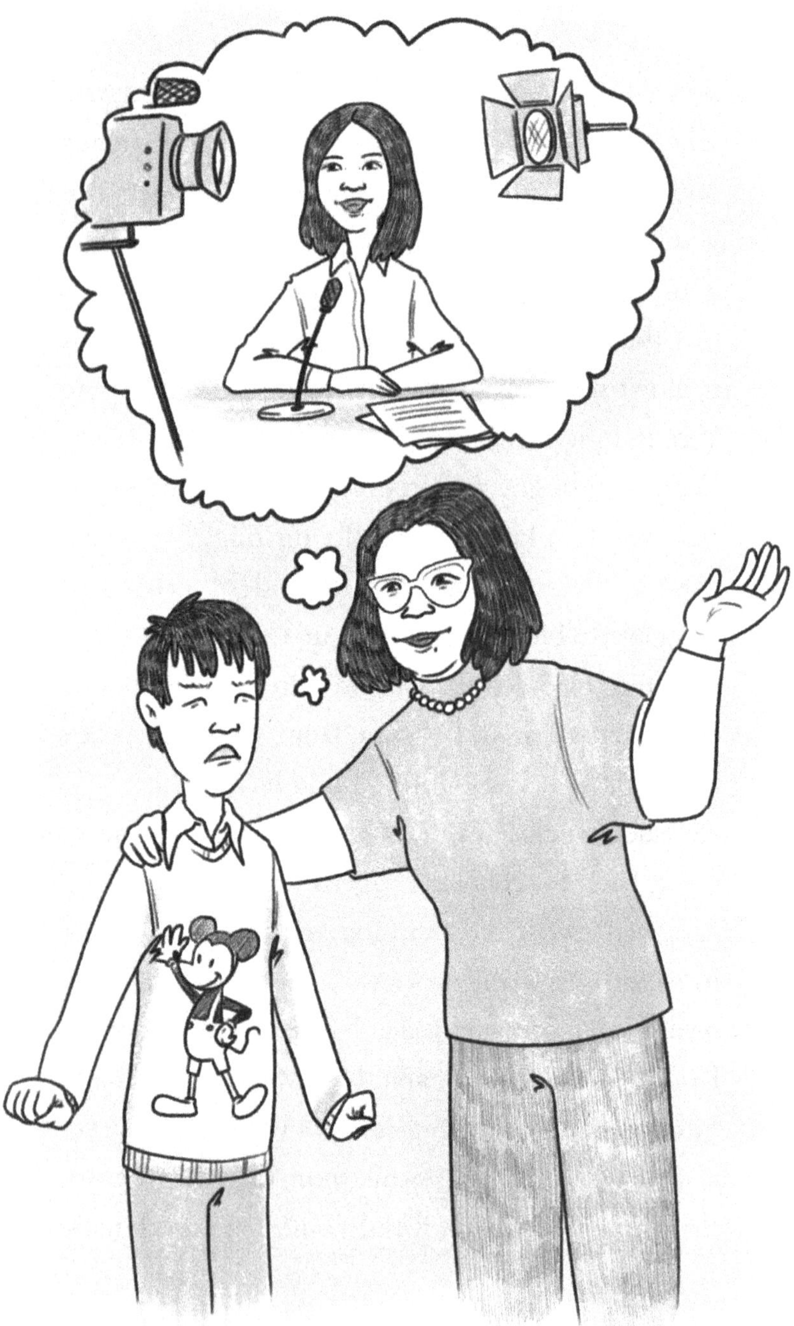

in 1974. When she'd first come to Australia, she'd taken up a job as a bookkeeping clerk – something to do with accounts and numbers for a small local business – but, back then, in Malaysia, Eddie's mum would have her hair and makeup done so that she could appear on camera, and she could speak 16 or 17 different languages like Mandarin, Cantonese and Malay. She met all sorts of amazing people. And she told funny stories about Eddie's dad's huge family and hers; about all the uncles, aunts and cousins – so many cousins – that Eddie had never met before because none of their extended family ever seemed to leave Malaysia. They were all still there. Except for the one time that his grandma on his dad's side had come to visit, and she was very stern. Eddie's mum's old life, and all their family, seemed very far away.

Eddie's mum also told him stories about how she'd met his dad. Because of the glamorous TV newsreader job, his mum had been looking for a place to live closer to her work. Since his dad had moved to Australia to study, Eddie's paternal grandmother (the stern one) had rented Eddie's dad's old bedroom out to Eddie's future mum!

On one of Eddie's dad's trips back to Kuala Lumpur to see his family during university holidays, he'd met Eddie's mum, 'And that was that,' she smiled. 'That's how we met.'

'I wish you'd never left there to come here!' Eddie said once. 'It would all have been different!'

'It might have been *different*,' his mum replied quietly. 'But it might not have been any easier if we'd stayed. We made the hard decision, after your dad finished university in Canberra and moved to Sydney to find work, for me to come and join him here because we thought your dad would have a chance at a better job, and that this would be a better place to raise our children. We left our old lives and all our family behind so that you, and your big brother Kevin, and your big sister Kylie, would have an easier life than we had, growing up. We know this country is going to be good to you, Eddie. And you'll do great things when you grow up. But you just have to get through school first.'

After all the wondrous and funny stories about a place, and people, he'd never seen, but was somehow connected to, Eddie usually felt a little bit calmer. 'But you don't speak any of those languages you know to *us*, Mum,' Eddie said once, puzzled. 'We mainly speak English at home. I can say my name, count and talk about food in Cantonese, but that's it.'

'We wanted you to grow up without accents,' his mum had replied, 'and have a much easier time than we did, coming here. We don't want you just to *live* here, *Boh*, we want you to *belong* here. And you do. And you will.'

On those really bad days, when Eddie dug his heels in and flatly refused to go to school, his mum would let him stay home with her, or tag around the shops with her, doing errands. While on those errands, his mum would often buy him books to cheer him up – like fantastic choose-your-own-adventure stories or the puzzle books that he would spend hours getting lost in, becoming a hero and a problem-solver instead of the *Loser* and *Dork* that the bullies liked to call him.

> **Racism** occurs when a person, community, institution (like a government, workplace or school) or system (like a legal system) treats someone badly because of their skin colour or ethnic background. It can take the form of abuse or violence, but it also includes name-calling, jokes and exclusion. Racism has terrible effects on individuals, and whole communities, because it can impact on a person's mental and physical health and their ability to achieve their future goals.

Eddie's absolute favourite puzzle books of all time were the *Usborne Puzzle Adventure* series which usually featured a blood-curdling adventure with a puzzle to solve on every page. Eddie probably owned every single one ever written and published. But loving those puzzle books only made things worse, because when he was sitting there at school poring over them, the other kids saw him as a *nerd* and different. Too different to leave alone.

On the very worst days, when life didn't seem worth leaving home for ever again, Eddie's mum would take him on a bus to Parramatta Library – which was way bigger than his library at school – where Eddie would sit and read all day, and forget about real life for a while.

3

It's okay to be an outsider

When Eddie arrived at school that morning it had seemed like it would be a good day. For once, there was no one waiting for him as he ran through the gates and he slid gratefully into his seat in his Year 3 classroom. He got stuck straight into the story he had to write for English, one of his favourite things to do of all time.

But at lunchtime, when Eddie was sitting on his own under a tree reading, a group of bigger boys from Years 5 and 6 kicked their ball over the school fence by mistake, nearby.

'Oi,' they shouted, '*Dork*'.

Eddie didn't look up. Engaging meant trouble, and he was going to pretend they were shouting at someone else. He hunched over his book, drawing his knees up under his chin, making himself even smaller than usual so that maybe they wouldn't notice him anymore and move onto someone else.

'Oi!' one of the boys said again more loudly, coming across and standing over Eddie, blocking out the sunlight. '*Nerd*. Get our ball!'

Eddie looked up from where he was sitting on the ground. The boy seemed enormous, and Eddie could feel the stares of the other boys in the gang and hear their sniggering and whispering. He knew all of them, and their fists, and all of them were *trouble*. Eddie shook his head knowing that any student who left the school grounds during school hours would catch it. It would be detentions, or worse.

'Do it,' the boy snarled, 'or I'll break your face'.

'No!' Eddie insisted. 'I'll get into trouble.'

'That's *the point*,' one of the other boys had laughed before they all jumped on Eddie, punching and kicking and pulling him around by his clothes until Eddie gave up and went outside the school gates to fetch their ball, sweating with fear the entire time. He threw the ball back over the fence to where they were waiting, and they ran off laughing. But as soon as Eddie re-entered the school, a teacher was waiting for him who immediately put Eddie on detention for leaving the school boundaries.

He tried to tell the teacher what had happened, but her face went all tight, closed and unfriendly in the same way his classroom teacher's face had changed when his eczema was being somehow 'disruptive' to the whole class.

Nobody ever wanted to listen it seemed, so from that day, Eddie started bottling things up more and more. Even though he spoke English just as well as every other kid at his school did, and sometimes felt just as 'Australian' inside, it didn't ever help. It wasn't even the beatings, isolation, mocking or loneliness that bothered him; it was that he didn't understand what the bullies really wanted or why they didn't just leave him alone. It was all such a waste of time and energy.

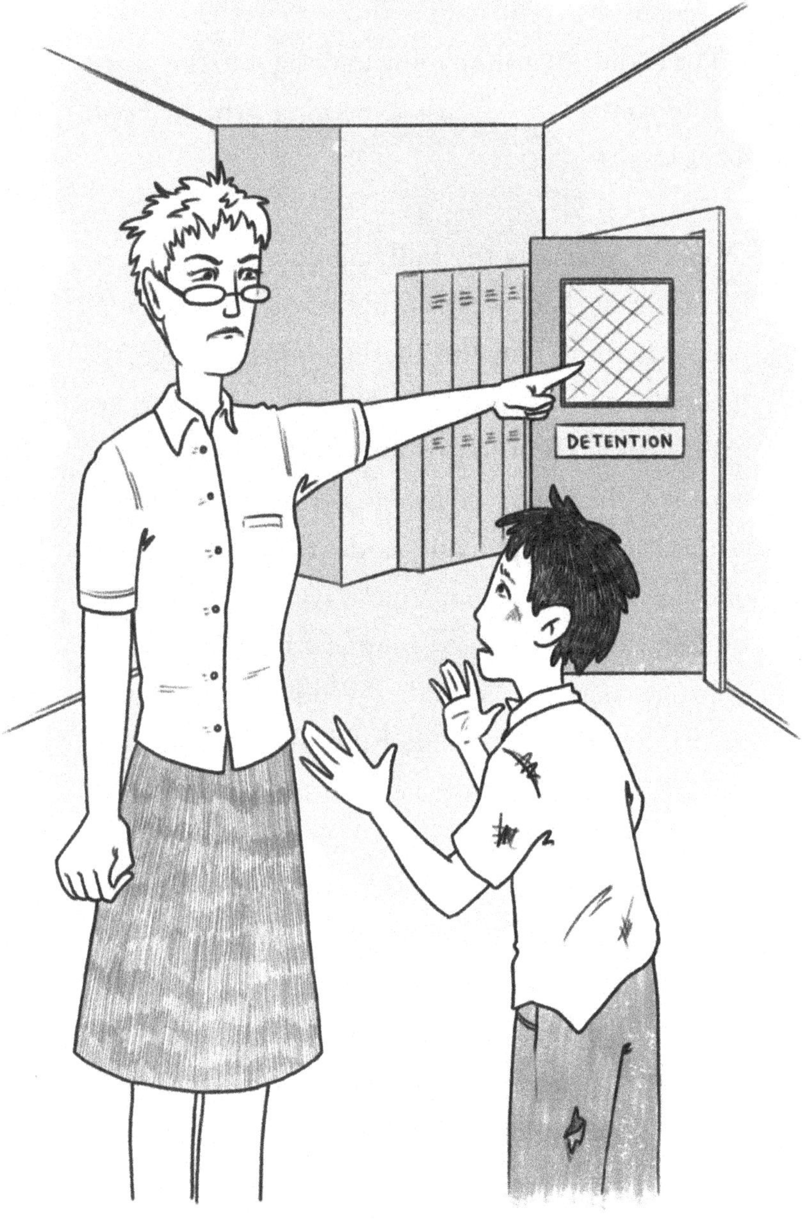
DETENTION

School wasn't just something to get through – Eddie couldn't even imagine making it to the other side of school – it was just something to be *survived*. That was all.

*

Over the years, as the bullying continued, Eddie learned that there was nothing he could do to stop people making him feel that he didn't belong. All he could do was 'grin and bear it' – a saying he really hated, because grinning had nothing to do with it – then get ready to go through it all again the next day. But it made Eddie really take notice of other kids in the playground who were just like him; who didn't have a group of friends or maybe even one friend to play with, the kids who inhabited the fringes, just like he did. Eddie usually spent his days alone, except when he was in class or had to join a team in PE or compete against someone in Chess Club, and he grew to be very observant.

Life started to change when Eddie entered Year 4. He found himself part of a 'composite class' that had a mix of Year 3, Year 4 and Year 6 students in it. As the teacher had to prepare work that would suit kids from a lot of different age groups, Eddie began to regularly do the Year 6 work for Literacy and Science, although he struggled a bit with the Maths. The kids in the class – ranging in age from 9 to 13 years – weren't any more accepting of Eddie than the kids he'd been through earlier years with. Eddie was still the only Chinese kid in his class, and that made him a target.

During that year, however, Eddie sat a test for entry into an 'Opportunity Class' or 'OC', which some New South Wales primary schools ran for academically gifted children in Years 5 and 6 – a two-year program to help students learn by grouping them with kids like them who loved to learn.

Until he sat that test, Eddie hadn't realised that his government primary school was one of those with an OC, and his test score was high enough that he qualified for entry! Getting into that class didn't mean that the bullying stopped. But the kids in the OC class were a little more like Eddie was. Learning was considered okay. Being an *outsider*, or even an *outlier* (a person quite different from others), was also okay. Eddie was now one of a handful of Asian kids in his class. It meant that, over those two final years of primary school, Eddie did start to feel more comfortable with who he was. He was suddenly surrounded, for the first time, by kids much more like him. Even scratching his eczema didn't seem to be so 'disruptive' anymore because other kids had it, too. He was more accepted by the other students and teachers, although he still didn't have people he could really call *friends*. All of his experiences over the last few years had made Eddie very quiet and wary around groups of any kind.

While Eddie started to feel less alone, he still had to run fast through the school gates and watch his back, and his stuff. The kids outside the OC never let up with their bullying – although they couldn't reach him when he was in class, they could still wait for him in the playground and at the gates.

*

During his terrible primary school years, when every day felt as if it went on for decades instead of hours, Eddie was developing this useful thing called *empathy*. He didn't know it yet, but empathy would become one of his superpowers one day. It would help him to become a kind, resilient and generous teacher, person, friend and father. But in the middle of kids endlessly stealing and destroying his things, and beating him up just for being who he was, Eddie didn't realise that.

> *Empathy* is a really important life skill which includes the ability to see something from another person's perspective or feel another person's emotions and take steps to help them if they are in pain.

4

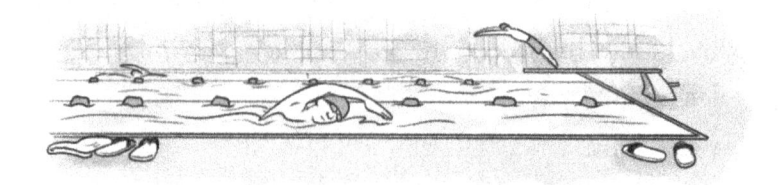

Getting stronger all the time

Being part of the 'Opportunity Class' or OC throughout Years 5 and 6 wasn't the only thing that was slowly changing Eddie's life. He was getting stronger in lots of other ways, both physically and spiritually.

Because of all the asthma attacks he was having, his family doctor recommended that Eddie do more swimming. So, when Eddie was in Year 2, he started swimming training at the local pool on Saturdays to make his lungs stronger and continued doing that until he was in Year 9. He was never the fastest or strongest swimmer, and it didn't make Eddie grow much taller or wider in the shoulders. But as the weeks went on, Eddie became a regular member of the swim squad. The best thing about training though, which finished around lunchtime, was his mum taking him to McDonald's afterwards for fries and a cheeseburger. The cheeseburgers never seemed to make Eddie any fatter or faster, but the amazing thing about all those years of swim training was that for over ten years after he stopped going to squad, whenever Eddie unwrapped a McDonald's cheeseburger, he could smell the chlorine smell of the public pool where he used to train! The mind is an amazing thing, because cheeseburgers and chlorine went together in Eddie's brain for a very long time.

Amazing brain fact!
Because of the way the human brain is structured, certain smells and/or tastes are closely linked to memory. Our brains can store positive or negative emotional memories for a long time – like Eddie's memory about cheeseburgers after swimming.

Eddie also attended church with his family on Sundays where the Woos caught up with an Asian (mostly Singaporean and Malaysian) community that came from all over Sydney for the service. At church, Eddie was able to enjoy a safe space where the person you were, rather than what you looked like, determined whether you had friends or respect. Eddie usually enjoyed sitting with the adults and listening to the sermons given by the pastor rather than attending Sunday School or craft lessons with his friends. Listening to all of the stories helped Eddie to feel like he was part of something bigger, something timeless, and also taught him greater empathy for others.

Another thing that helped Eddie recharge was playing computer games with his older brother, Kevin, who was eight years older than Eddie and really funny, goofy, kind and patient.

> In many Asian cultures, children and young people are likely to call older men 'Uncle' and older women 'Aunty', as a sign of respect, affection, relationship or connection – even if they aren't related to them.

By the time Eddie was in Year 5, Kevin was already studying a software engineering degree at university. Eddie did sometimes tell Kevin and Kylie a little about what he was going through, and they empathised a lot because they'd experienced discrimination, too – but Kylie and Kevin had always had a wide circle of friends and been more accepted because they were more outgoing than Eddie. Kevin played team sports like rugby, and Kylie was often at her friends' houses or working at the local fruit shop on the weekends, so it was hard for them to really understand what Eddie was going through or how isolated he felt.

Knowing this, Kevin tried his hardest to be a great friend and mentor to Eddie. Eddie loved playing two-player games with his brother where each of them would control a character (like a ninja, a beefy, bare-chested warrior or an axe-wielding troll), the characters working co-operatively to fight baddies, complete levels and defeat the ultimate bad guy at the end of the game. Eddie and Kevin would sit together for hours, laughing and conquering multi-level games like *Ninja Gaiden*, *Silkworm*, *Midnight Resistance*, *Final Fight* and *Golden Axe*.

Because Eddie's fingers were so short – too short for him to continue with piano lessons according to Eddie's ex-piano teacher! – Kevin would use the keys on the left-hand side of the computer keyboard while Eddie would use the ones on the right (because they had arrows and were easier to read). When they reached certain parts of the harder levels where Eddie couldn't press the correct buttons fast enough to get his character to do the right things, Kevin would reach over to Eddie's side and do it for him so that they could keep progressing through the adventure together. Eddie loved the time he got to spend with his busy, older brother. It was also a lot more fun bashing cartoon baddies with his brother than playing computer games on his own.

Being an avid computer programmer, Kevin also patiently taught Eddie everything he knew about technology, computers and music. One day, when Eddie got old enough to learn, Kevin would even teach Eddie how to drive a car! To this day, Eddie and Kevin share the same sense of humour and love the same kinds of TV shows and music.

Kylie was the kind of no-nonsense, hardworking older sister who listened and gave good advice, the rare times when she was home. She was five years older than Eddie whom she called him *Ez*, and would tell him it was okay to like learning things because she liked learning things, too. Kylie had gone to a selective school for the final two years of high school after working really hard to get in. To their parents' dismay, Kylie had actually turned down a place at the selective high school in Year 8 because she didn't want to leave her close group of friends at her old school. But when she realised that she'd learn even more at the high school she'd turned down, Kylie had studied hard to win a place there all over again. That was the kind of person she was. She just got on with things and was usually working hard at something, or socialising.

'You know that Mum and Dad put a big emphasis on education, Ez,' she would tell him. 'They want us to study hard so that we can do things and achieve stuff that they never could. The ability to learn new things is something that will stand you in good stead for the rest of your life. Don't be afraid of working hard, or of being who you are. I've been there too, I get it, little bro.'

It meant that when Eddie was at swim squad or at church or with his family, he hardly ever felt 'different', 'weird', 'nerdy' or a 'loser'. Eddie found that the things he did on the weekends, and the people he spent time with then, gave him the much-needed energy to face the difficult school week ahead.

*

When Eddie was in Year 6, all the students in his Opportunity Class were encouraged to sit a test to enter a government-funded selective high school (a school for academically gifted students) from Year 7 onwards. Being rich or tall, beefy or 'Australian' didn't help you get into those schools – only the way you thought and expressed yourself did. James Ruse Agricultural High (a school with an enormous farm, where you could learn agriculture as an actual subject!) was the most academically successful selective school in New South Wales and everyone in the OC wanted to go there.

Like the other kids in the OC, Eddie had to choose which selective school he wanted to go to if he could get a high enough test score. It wasn't a scholarship, as all the selective high schools were public schools that didn't require you to pay a lot of money to attend them. But Eddie wanted to get into James Ruse Agricultural High not because he'd get to manage land or animals, although that might be kind of interesting (he'd never done that before), but because it was the best selective high school in the whole of New South Wales, and possibly even the whole of Australia. Eddie wanted to show everyone he could do it. Both girls and boys could go there and it had been ranked first out of all the schools in the State for years and years. The kids who went there didn't have to apologise for liking reading or learning, and most of them came from

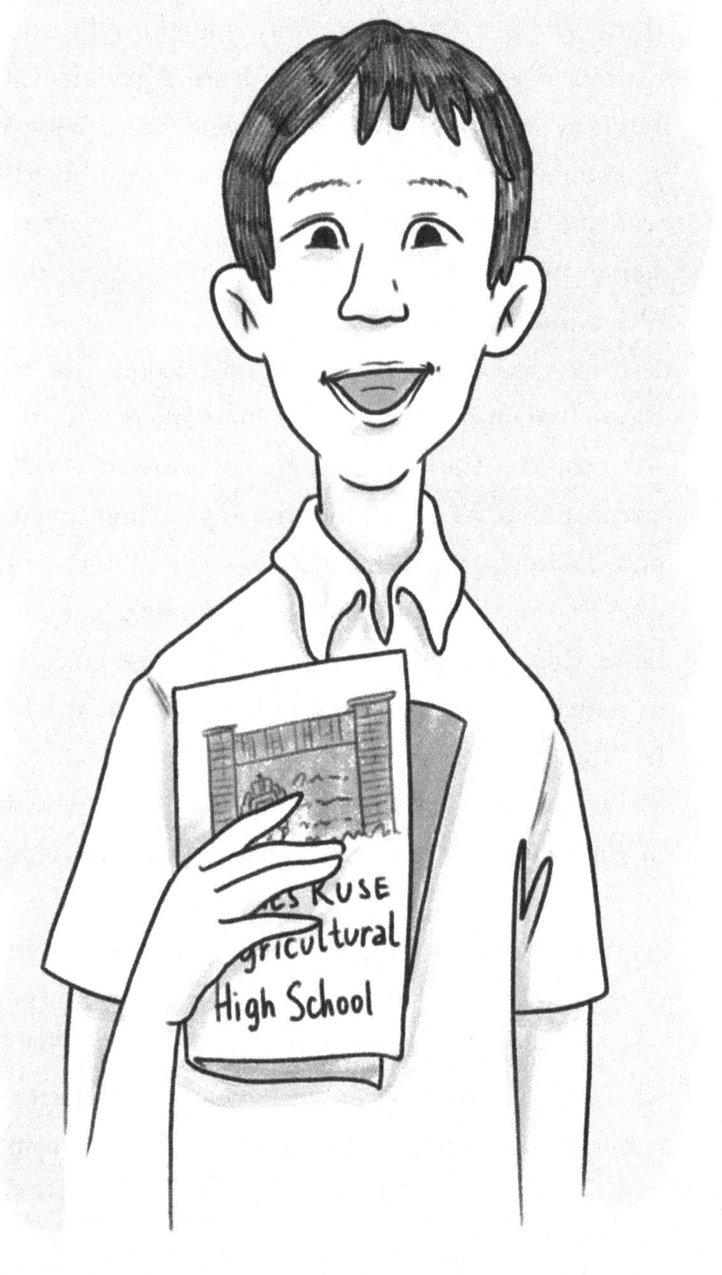
High School

backgrounds like Eddie's – non-English speaking backgrounds.

The school sounded like heaven, and the opposite of the 'White Australia' policy Eddie's dad had once told him about. After all these years of being told by the people at his primary school that he didn't belong, Eddie was hoping to get a place at a high school where people like him were actually *welcome*. The bullies who'd made all his years at primary school unbearable weren't going to be there because they never studied, paid attention or thought ahead to how they wanted their lives to turn out – they just picked fights with other people and never did their homework. He wanted to be in the company of even more people who actually enjoyed learning, the same way that he did.

Eddie hadn't grown that much since the bullies started messing with his things and his life, but his mind had grown a lot over the years. He'd always loved writing, and Eddie had kept journals, all through his primary school years, that involved him just writing page after page of things he was thinking about and things that he'd learned. Eddie wrote to process and understand all the things that had happened to him because, when he wrote things down, he found that it helped to make more sense out of what was going on.

All the reading he'd done in the time he'd spent on his own, all the processing of things that had happened to him and to the other bullied kids at school, all the endless laps at the pool and the fellowship, sacrifice, ancient stories and wisdom in the sermons he listened to every week, had made him wiser about how the world and people worked. Eddie didn't know it, but he was storing all his life experiences and accumulated knowledge away for later. Everything that had happened to him so far – good and bad – was making him into the adult he would be one day.

'The people who come out of that James Ruse High School,' said Eddie's dad after they talked about Eddie's choice of selective school at home, 'are *leaders*. Things like lawyers, engineers, politicians. It will be hard work, Eddie. Getting in, as well as going there.'

Eddie knew that his mum and dad would be so proud of him if he could just make it through the entrance exam and get a place at James Ruse.

All the sacrifices they made would be worth it, if that happened.

'I have to get in,' he told himself fiercely. 'Everything will change if I can just get in.'

Eddie knew he'd survived all those years at primary school for a reason. He was going to leave the bullies behind at last. But to do that, he had to study, study, *study*.

5

'Maths is not really my thing'

What Eddie remembered most about the entrance exam when people asked him about it afterwards was the loud ticking of the clock and how one corner of his desk wobbled. The exam was at the local high school near Eddie's home, in the large school hall there, and the wait before the exam had felt really long. There were crowds of people milling around outside; students from all different schools across the State had come to sit the test.

Eddie had felt like a wound-up spring ready to be let go. Sensing his nerves, his mum had hugged him tight and wished him, 'Good luck!' Eddie could tell she was just as nervous as he was because she really hoped he would do well, knowing that it would be life-changing for her son.

Inside the big hall the air had smelled like dust and tickled his nose mercilessly throughout the exam. As soon as they could start writing, Eddie pushed aside the butterflies in his stomach and wrote like a fury. He wrote so fast his wrist hurt and there were ink and pressure marks on the ends of his fingers after they were told to stop writing. The words had flowed from his pen, and the three hours it took to decide his future went by in a blur. Once he'd overcome his initial nerves, Eddie had really enjoyed solving the puzzles and answering the questions in the paper. They'd reminded him, in a way, of his cherished Usborne Puzzle Adventure books. He'd known deep inside that he had a chance. He'd worked hard. He'd made sure his writing wasn't too messy! But he hadn't felt confident, just incredibly nervous, in the lead up to the exam.

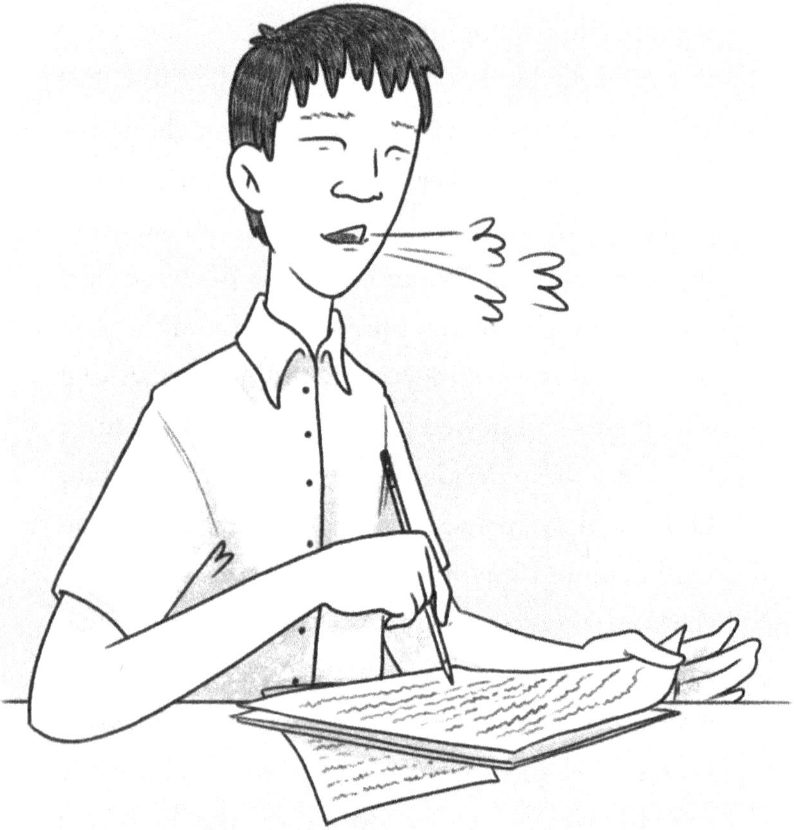

*

'What did you write about, *Boh?*' his mum asked him afterwards, but Eddie couldn't really remember.

'It seemed like the longest exam of my life, but also the fastest. It's kind of hard to explain,' Eddie told his parents in the car on the way home.

Waiting for the test result was the worst. No one at Eddie's primary school other than the kids in his Opportunity Class – not his old teachers, not the bullies – realised that he was waiting for something that might change his whole life, or how agonising that waiting was.

It took about three or four months before the results came through, and Eddie had almost forgotten about the exam completely when his family received a letter in the mail with an offer from James Ruse in it! Eddie had almost finished Year 6 when he arrived home from school one afternoon to the amazing news.

'You did it, *Boh*!' his mum beamed, hugging him.

'Did what?' Eddie was momentarily confused as his mum held out the letter to him.

As soon as he saw the letterhead with the name 'James Ruse' on it, his face cleared. 'I'm in!' he yelled delightedly, punching the air. 'Yessssss!'

Eddie could feel his dad's pride that night at the dinner table as his mum recounted the contents of the letter to Kevin and Kylie.

'You're going to love high school, Ez,' Kylie smiled, who was in her final year at school. 'It's a whole new world. There's so much to do!'

'It's like one of our computer games,' Kevin grinned. 'You've smashed through all the trolls and made it to the ultimate bad guy levels!'

Eddie ate dinner that night feeling enormous relief and an incredible hope. *He'd got a place at James Ruse Agricultural High School.* His escape pod was waiting. Everything would be different when he got to high school next year. It was a chance to start again with new people. To maybe be the person that he was meant to be.

Eddie's family celebrated when he got in because both Kevin and Kylie had sat the same kind of difficult test but neither of them had gone to a selective school from Year 7 onwards like Eddie would be doing. Those kinds of tests were tough.

It was amazing what Eddie had achieved given how hard his experience of school had been until now. Two other kids from Eddie's OC class that he got along well with also gained places at James Ruse which meant that at least there would be a couple of faces he recognised on his first day.

'There will be a lot of pressure to do well and a lot of competition at James Ruse,' his parents warned Eddie. 'You'll need to work hard, be organised and stay focused.'

But Eddie was just looking forward to a school that had more cool subjects, more facilities and new people in it that he could start afresh with. Eddie was really looking forward to having *choices*.

*

His first day was exciting and exhausting. He felt overwhelmed by how big it was and didn't think he would ever remember anyone's name or where to go for classes. All summer, Eddie had been fizzing with excitement inside to be making a fresh start. Sure, the OC had given Eddie a taste of being among people who understood him better and who he could get along with, but Eddie wanted to make real friends and go to a school with lots of subject choices and bigger and better facilities.

One thing he hadn't looked forward to was wearing the compulsory school blazer that had stared out at him from his wardrobe during the summer holidays – it looked so formal, stiff, uncomfortable and imposing. He couldn't imagine having to put that on every day! Because it had been quite expensive to buy, Eddie's mum had wanted to make sure that the blazer she bought would last a long time. So the one she bought was about two sizes too big so that Eddie could 'grow into it'. Just about every item of clothing in Eddie's wardrobe was way too big for him, for exactly this reason. The few times that he'd tried the blazer on over summer, Eddie had yelled out to his mum, 'I feel like a duck!' because of the blazer's overlong, flappy sleeves.

But the best thing about his new school was making friends straight away with a group of three other boys, two Sri Lankan boys and a Caucasian guy, who were in all of his classes and also caught the same bus as him. But that first day, Eddie spent a lot of it either terrified or laughing. For the first time in his life, he felt as if he truly *belonged* somewhere.

By the end of his first week at the high school, Eddie felt as if he'd finally found his tribe. Girls had been a completely intimidating mystery in primary school, but he'd even started *speaking* to them at James Ruse and, eventually, his new circle of friends included boys *and* girls (Eddie would even meet his future wife there!). There were people like him in high school, but a whole range of people who weren't, and that was totally okay, too. There was a 'popular' group, a 'basketball' group and a whole bunch of other groups made up of people from a whole range of classes with a wide spectrum of interests. But no one, no matter what group they belonged to, stole things out of his school bag, or beat him up for fun. Instead, people were curious, friendly, funny and respectful. It was fine to ask questions, just as it was fine to be a nerd who hung out at the library and wasn't that good at sport (whose general enthusiasm more than made up for a lack of ball skills!). James Ruse was a real *Live-and-Let-Live* kind of school, where being yourself and pursuing your own interests were encouraged. That suited Eddie down to the ground after his experiences at primary school.

The school's policy was to have older kids assigned to look after Year 7 students, which made a huge impression on Eddie – that people were there just to make sure he was doing fine. To answer all his questions, and he had plenty, and be a shoulder to lean on. Suddenly, school was *fun* and *exciting* in a way it hadn't been before. It wasn't hard to get out of bed anymore and he didn't need to hide his love of reading, writing and learning new things. While Eddie and his parents didn't really talk about icky things like *emotions*, they could tell that Eddie was much, much happier. Eddie never even talked about hiding out at Parramatta Library anymore, which was a huge relief to his mum. Eddie was even managing to control his own allergies a lot better and didn't even scratch as much! And he just felt ... lighter.

Eddie still found Maths a struggle though – it didn't come naturally to him at all and he could never make it into the best Maths class, not even the second-best Maths class (there were eight!). Maybe the fifth or sixth-best Maths class at most. But he could read and write and use his voice as much as he liked in the English, History and Drama classes that he absolutely loved. He also threw himself into mentoring and coaching younger kids as he got older: he joined the Australian Army Cadets in Year 8 and helped with community service projects like Amnesty International in Year 10. Because James Ruse was an *agricultural* high school, Eddie also did farming subjects at school, something he'd never imagined being able to do before at his old primary school that had mostly been surrounded by asphalt and concrete. Because of Eddie's allergies and eczema, he'd never even had a pet dog or cat as a kid. Just one fish, the whole of the time he was growing up, called *Steve*. His eczema was also more manageable by this stage because there were better medicines at hand and he had better self-control. Everything, even his skin, was looking up!

Eddie studied agriculture both while at the school – which had its own huge school farm! – and at places like the Sydney Royal Easter Show and farms as far away as Bathurst and Gloucester in New South Wales that they had to take buses out to. Through teachers like Mr Lisle Brown, who literally wrote a textbook on farming, Eddie took part in practical agriculture lessons which involved things like growing vegetables, fruit and flowers outside and in glasshouses, and also looking after livestock like cows, sheep, chickens and fish, and the health of local waterways.

He'd never been a super outdoorsy person or felt comfortable around plants or animals before, but Eddie started getting his hands dirty and he found that he *loved* it. Although not the one time in Year 8 when he arrived late to the outdoor classroom in

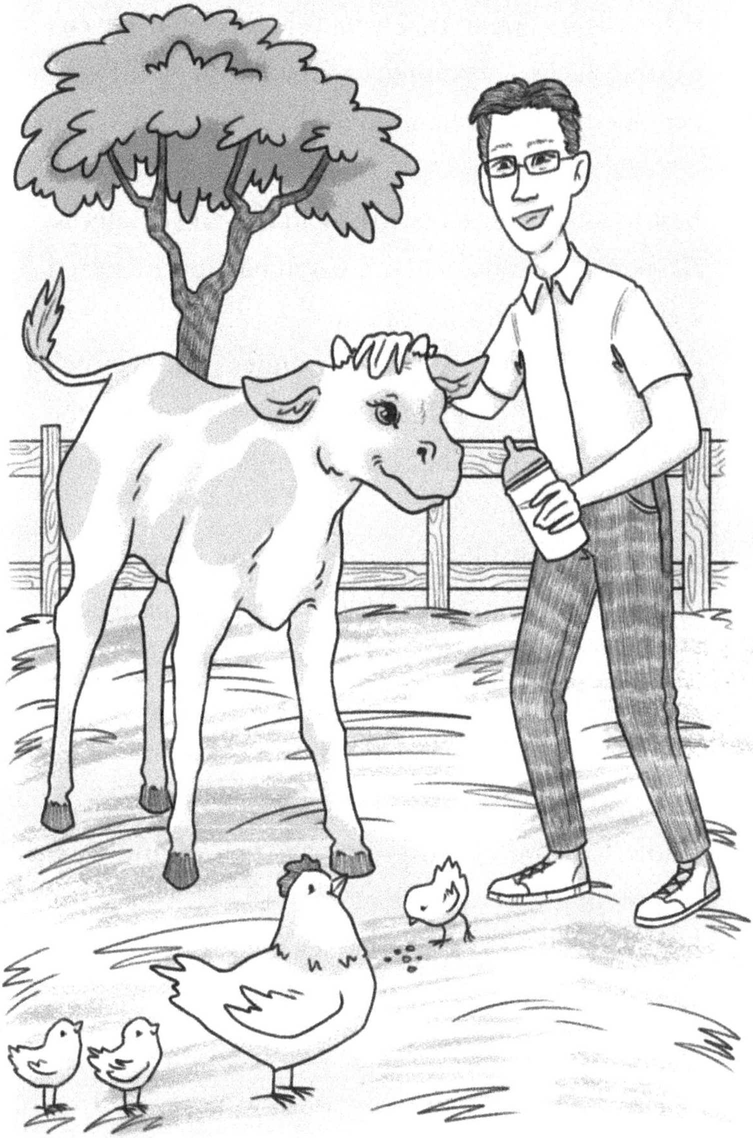

the middle of an Agriculture lesson. The teacher, Mr Arnison, had greeted Eddie casually with 'Oh, Edward, it's great that you're here – you haven't missed the important part of the lesson at all!' and extended his right hand to shake Eddie's.

As Eddie shook Mr Arnison's hand, doing his best to look his teacher firmly in the eye, the entire class groaned loudly. Mr Arnison had just dissected a chicken with his bare hands!

'Gotcha!' Mr Arnison grinned, to Eddie's confusion. When Eddie found out later about the chicken dissection, he felt as if he needed a shower, not just a handwash!

High school also let Eddie learn things at so much more depth than he'd ever experienced before, and he embraced all the extra-curricular activities that he could fit into his already busy schedule. After a short-lived and disastrous stint learning the piano in primary school – which Eddie had found hard and inaccessible and a bit of a struggle, kind of like Maths – he picked up new creative pursuits at James Ruse like Graphic Design and Digital Art. Eddie spent hours creating artwork on his computer featuring the enormous, complicated spaceships from one of his favourite Sci-Fi space simulator games; which let you fly spaceships around and shoot aliens. Eddie was learning so much about new things that he'd never dreamed of before and his mind continued to grow. He was getting taller, too!

Eddie also developed a love of photography, pleading with his parents until they bought him a very early model digital camera. It quickly became Eddie's most treasured possession while he was growing up, and he took it everywhere, creating websites filled with photos of his friends and funny notes about things that they'd done together, like the Sydney City2Surf run. This was in the days before Facebook even existed!

Amazingly, Eddie – a kid who used to hide from the bullies and even some of his teachers – found himself taking up Drama, with his parents' encouragement, as an elective subject and ended up loving presenting plays in front of large groups of people. Eddie had begged to do Graphic Design and in return his parents – who knew how shy Eddie was – had agreed, but only if he'd consider taking up Drama because they thought it might help him to speak up more and be more outgoing. He also became a leader in the school's Christian group – discovering that he liked helping others to learn, and that he had a gift for explaining complex things and ideas in simple terms that came alive for people.

It felt as if life couldn't get any better or more different than it was before. It felt like, finally, Eddie was getting everything that he wanted out of school.

Little did Eddie know that life was going to throw up more, and even harder, tests in his near future.

6

The fight of her life

It had never occurred to Eddie before high school that teachers would *care* about him. One day, on a long walk down to the school farm Mr Brown, the agriculture teacher turned to him and asked, 'Edward, how are you *doing* today?'

Eddie froze in surprise, remembering the teachers at his primary school who'd never seemed to see him at all, not even when he was being pummelled right under their noses. But when they did see him, it was usually to send him to the Principal's office for punishment.

Eddie had never been asked a question like that by an adult outside his family or church group before. His first thoughts were, *Is this a test? How do I answer?*

But Mr Brown actually meant it. He really wanted to know; he cared whether Eddie was happy, physically *and* mentally. Seeing that teachers cared for their students and saw their students as individual people, not just as a big mob of annoying, noisy kids who were all the same, made a really deep impression on Eddie. It made him feel as if he counted. That he was important. That he was *seen*. Eddie's world view suddenly shifted.

Mr Best, the music teacher, wasn't even supposed to notice students like Eddie, who'd pretty much been kicked out of piano lessons by his primary school piano teacher. But Mr Best cared about how Eddie was doing, too, and always asked after him as well. For the first time, it felt as if his teachers weren't just there to talk *at* Eddie, they were there to talk *with* Eddie. To be mentors and friends, as well as teachers. The tiny seed already in Eddie's mind – that had something to do with supporting others with kindness and empathy – began to really grow.

Eddie soon grew used to having lots of conversations with teachers after class or just walking around the playground. Because he liked learning, he was often curious about things he'd heard in a teacher's lesson or had read about in the library so he would often ask a teacher on his way out of class, or in the playground, to go into more detail about something that had caught his interest. Most of Eddie's teachers relished talking about subjects they were very passionate about, and Eddie found himself seeing a lot of his subjects in a new light. Subjects like English and History were more than just the set tasks the students were being given, he realised. Talking about them in-depth made those subjects really come alive for him.

But try as hard as he could, Eddie still didn't *love* Maths. He loved almost everything else about high school but not Maths – it just wasn't his thing. He could do it, *just*, but it was hard. Luckily, he had a good memory, because he didn't love having to remember the complicated formulae he needed to solve abstract problems that seemed to have no bearing on his life. Maths didn't fire his imagination like English, Drama, Photography,

Graphic Design or History did. School let Eddie do cool things like shoot, script write and edit his own short movies! If Eddie could have studied 1,000 subjects at school he would have. He'd always been an intensely curious and omnivorous learner. Just not about Maths.

When Eddie was at James Ruse Agricultural High, school wasn't about Maths at all. Maths was just something he did on the side of everything else. Maths was something he got through; just like the bullying he'd endured when he was younger.

*

Although things at school were going really well, Eddie's mum began to feel pain when she was breathing and her chest and ribs started to hurt all the time. Then she developed a constant cough and was getting thinner and more tired, every day.

At night, the rest of the family could hear her coughing in her sleep. She'd always been a fit and healthy person.

'You should go and see someone, Mum,' Eddie, Kevin and Kylie would urge her.

'Nonsense,' Angela would reply. 'It's just a cough. It will go away all by itself.'

Eddie's dad finally had to drag his mum off to see the doctor, who quickly sent her off to see a range of specialists.

It was a huge shock to the whole Woo family when the diagnosis came back from the specialists – Eddie's mum had lung cancer.

Eddie was in Year 10 when they found out, and it felt as if the floor had fallen out from under his feet. His mum was the heart and core of the family. Even if Eddie was squabbling with Kylie, or Kevin was so busy with work that he was spending less time with Eddie, each of their relationships with their mum stayed strong and nurturing. She was just always *there* – ready with food or a kind word at any time of the day when her husband, or one of her kids, would burst through the door.

When Eddie thought about the word *cancer*, he thought of really old people (his mum was only 51 years old) or people who ate a box of iced doughnuts every day washed down with litres of sugary drink. He couldn't understand how his mum could have lung cancer when she'd never even picked up a cigarette in her life.

Eddie knew that his mum was afraid, but she never said it out loud because she didn't want to burden any of them with her fear. All she'd say was, 'We'll get through this, you'll see'.

Eddie's mum was a tough fighter, but the treatment seemed to be worse than the cancer itself. She went through months of things like chemotherapy (where strong anti-cancer drugs are injected straight into your body) and radiation therapy (using strong radiation to control or kill cancer cells) but the cancer was very advanced when the doctors discovered it and it continued to quickly spread throughout her body.

Throughout all the specialists' appointments and hospital visits, Eddie felt intense confusion. It reminded him a little of the time he'd gone on a kayaking school camp and capsized in a rough current. He'd tried to tread water, but the current was just too strong and unpredictable, and he'd felt as if he was being swept away, just struggling to keep his head above the surface to breathe, or he'd drown. But his mum's cancer was far, far worse than that. Eddie felt a lot like he was going under and might never come up again.

Angela was only given months to live. By this time, Kevin had just started an important job at an IT company and Kylie was in her final year of university studying to be a dentist and doing loads of exams. Eddie's dad, who was a tax accountant, had to downsize his business and reduce his working hours so that he had more time to care for Eddie's mum.

But Eddie could see how the physical and emotional drain of looking after his mum was also wearing his dad down. Eddie knew that because he was still just in high school, and not doing things as important as his dad and his siblings, it was up to him to try to help his dad care for his mum. While Eddie's dad took care of the hospital and doctors' appointments and updating Angela's large circle of friends during the day, Eddie began to take on all of the night shifts.

As the cancer accelerated, and Eddie's mum steadily lost the ability to breathe without help, she started to need her oxygen tank even while she was asleep. Eddie began to sit by her bed at all hours of the night – like 11 p.m., 1 a.m. and 3 a.m. – to change her oxygen tank and be ready, at a moment's notice, to bring her whatever she needed. He volunteered without complaining because he knew that his brother, sister and dad needed to be able to get through their busy days and that they were all struggling with the sadness and the consequences of his mum's illness.

Eddie could see his family falling apart around him, so he knew that he had to be strong and try to hold them all together. But it also meant that he often fell asleep in the middle of the day during class, which completely puzzled his friends because his mum hadn't wanted Eddie to tell any of them that she had cancer. She was a very private person. Plus, she hadn't wanted Eddie to be known as *That kid whose mum has cancer*. She remembered how Eddie had been singled out as 'different' during his primary school days and she didn't want that happening again in high school.

It really helped that Eddie's teachers *did* care about him though. After Eddie told a few of them about what was going on at home – to explain why his homework was sometimes late, and why he was so distracted or tired during lessons – they would often tell the other students in his class to leave Eddie alone in the corner of the room while he slept with his head on his desk.

Other times, the teachers would send Eddie to the sick bay where he could squeeze in a couple of hours of sleep before waking in the afternoon and going home to sit up with his mum all night again. But it did mean that Eddie's marks began to drop all the way through to the end of Year 12 as his mum's fight with cancer became even more severe. Being a steady rock for his family meant that Eddie was just getting by at school. Every day seemed impossible. And then he'd have to get up and do everything all over again.

His future was on the line. But it was more important to Eddie that he be there for his family, especially his dad, who was doing it really tough. His dad had always been a reserved man who never spoke about his feelings which meant that he was bottling up all his sorrow and silently suffering throughout his wife's illness.

'Hang in there, Dad,' Eddie would tell him, gripping him by the shoulders. 'You'll be all right.'

But inside, Eddie himself was a mess. Through all the upheaval, he still needed to decide what he wanted to do after he left school. Would he even get a place at university the way things were going?

Plus, Eddie's dad wanted him to do a course at university that would earn him a lot of money and 'set him up for life'; maybe give him more 'status' than Eddie's parents ever had – something like law or medicine. Occupations Eddie wasn't the slightest bit interested in.

Instead, taking a deep breath one night, Eddie told his parents, 'I'm going to choose education. I want to be a *teacher*.' He was 17 years old.

The air was heavy after Eddie said that. Kevin and Kylie looked at each other across the dinner table. You really could cut the air with a knife or hear a pin drop. They knew that their parents had placed a lot of hope on Eddie becoming someone grander and more important than all of them, some day. It really mattered to them. They really had given up a lot for their kids.

His parents had looked at each other, too.

'What did you say?' Eddie's mum whispered, who was really ill at this stage. 'No, *Boh*, not teaching. Over my dead body.'

'Mum!' Eddie exclaimed in horror. 'Take that back!'

Eddie's dad asked him to think about his decision carefully.

'Why do you think we came to this country, Eddie? What do you think was the purpose for us leaving behind our families, our friends and our old life? Did you think we came here for the weather, or for the politics? To be called names and suffer racism? So that you could become a *teacher*?'

Eddie explained that everything he'd been through – at primary school, at James Ruse High, even now through his mum's illness – showed him that he wanted to help and support people.

'But I especially want to help them to *learn*,' Eddie insisted. 'Learning has brought me great joy and opportunity and I want to pass that joy on to other kids who might feel the same way I did when I was just coming out of primary school – confused and lonely. I want to give back one day, to *pay it forward*.' Eddie had always been an introvert, but high school, and his teachers' and friends' care and interest in him, had meant that he had gained a lot of confidence. Eddie wanted kids like he used to be, to feel that way, too.

'Perhaps the thing that I love most about James Ruse is that when I reached Year 11 this year and became a peer support mentor to younger kids, I could give the new kids the feeling of safety and belonging that I'd never had during my primary school years,' Eddie explained to his family. 'I still remember how I felt when I arrived at James Ruse – without any friends at all, or any good memories of school. The kind and caring older students who took me under their wing in my first year made such a huge impression on me. That's the feeling I want to pass on. I get real joy out of mentoring younger students.'

Eddie could see that his family was listening to him intently. No one was remembering to eat.

'The same way those older kids looked after me when I started high school,' Eddie reminded them, 'I've started mentoring my own group of Year 7s, Dad. And it's really made a difference to them, and to me. I'm a school prefect now. Teaching is what I want to do. *Teaching matters*, Mum and Dad. It can change lives. It changed mine.'

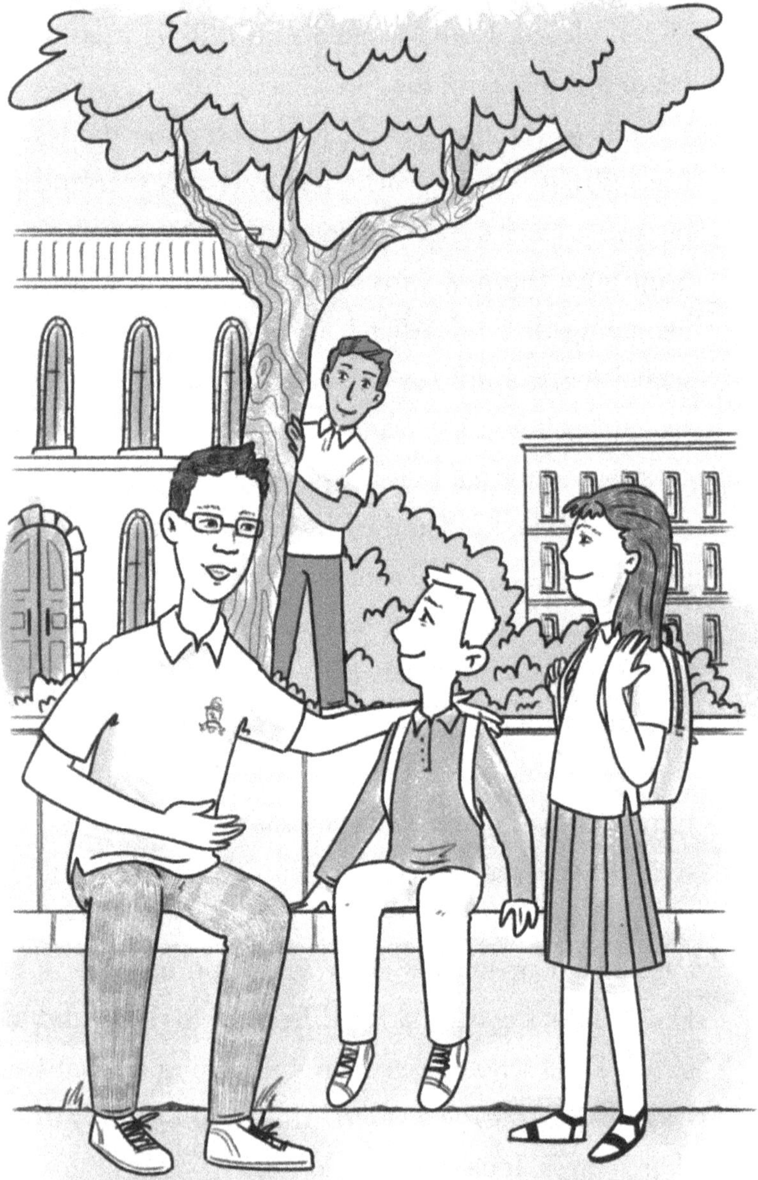

Finally, Eddie's dad said, 'Even though I don't understand your decision, I can see that it's very important to you.'

'It will change the course of your life, *Boh*,' his mum whispered. 'I hope you've thought very carefully about this.' Eddie knew that his mum was not going to stop him – she'd never held any of her children back from making their own decisions and sticking with them. But Eddie could almost *feel* her sadness. She had not seen teaching in his future at all.

'I have, Mum,' Eddie replied firmly. 'This is the path I want to take.'

Eddie's dad turned to his wife and said, 'Just let it be, let him do what he wants'.

But he reminded Eddie sternly, 'Whatever you do end up doing in life, you should just try to do your best, and be as good at it as you can.'

Not long after, Eddie sat his final Year 12 exams in English, Maths, Agriculture, Modern History, History and Drama; and then his mum passed away.

*

If you ask Eddie to describe his mum now, he would say that the one word – *warm* – perfectly encapsulated what she was like. When you were with her, there would be a feeling of softness or kindness; that you were in a safe and welcoming place. Eddie likes to think that he got his openness, warmth, approachability and deep sense of empathy, in large part, from his mum.

Angela was a really good friend to people all her life and had always kept a wide circle of friends because she was very caring and giving. She had had an innate sense of the value of human beings, which she'd tried to pass on to her children, and her absence felt like a giant crater had opened up inside the Woo household. It felt, at the time, like they were no longer really a family without her.

On the day of the funeral, Eddie tried to distract himself from his enormous loss by staying busy, and there was a lot to do. There were places to be at specific times, there was a multitude of tasks to do to make sure the service ran smoothly. There were so many people to shake hands with and talk to, and Eddie found it draining and difficult, just like his sister, brother and father did. But he knew it was important to put on a brave face and also to show everyone how grateful the whole family was for people coming to celebrate Angela's life with them and being there to support them.

Because Eddie had never told his friends about his mum's cancer, he had to explain to all of them who attended the funeral, for the first time, that his mum had been sick for several years and that was why he had fallen asleep in class, or seemed distant or distracted, over the last couple of years of high school. After the funeral was over though, and all the mourners had gone home and it was just Eddie, his dad, his sister and his brother left in the house, the enormity of their loss really hit home. She was really gone, and the fact she would stay gone, and not be there to cheer them all on for the rest of their lives, settled on them like a heavy weight. The grief seemed unbearable.

Even though he was still a teenager, his mum's dying caused Eddie to grow up really fast. Soon afterwards, Eddie's brother and sister moved out of home to start their adult lives. As they were a lot older than him, and already making their way in their chosen careers, he never felt resentful of them leaving, or felt abandoned. But it *was* hard. Eddie's dad was still heartbroken and Eddie, even though he'd always been the 'baby' of the family, found himself comforting and taking care of his dad, as well as himself.

If you'd asked Eddie at the time what impact his mum's death had had on him, his final exams, his family, his sense of security, his sense of the world, he would probably say that *every* part of his personality and outlook on life was affected by what had happened with his mum. It made him even slower to judge other people – even if they were rude or abrupt or angry – because he knew that there would be things going on in their lives that he simply couldn't see. The same way that his closest friends never even knew how ill Eddie's mother was; only finding out the real reason behind his falling asleep all over the school when Eddie invited them to her funeral. Someone had once told Eddie to, *Be kind, for everyone you meet is fighting a hard battle.*

His own experiences told Eddie that this was very likely to be *true*.

7

A chance encounter

In the same way that his mum's illness and death had a profound effect on Eddie's empathy for others, especially those with an illness, they also had a profound effect on Eddie's faith. Believing that he would see his mum again one day helped him to deal with the big questions constantly crowding his mind like: *Why do bad things happen to innocent people? Why is my grief so deep if death is just a part of life? What is the meaning of all my heartache? How do I hold on to hope when the world seems so dark?*

His faith, his belief that he was part of something bigger, contributed to Eddie taking a huge leap of faith on his first day at the University of Sydney. He was the only student from his year level at James Ruse who had chosen to study teaching at university. Eddie was standing in a long queue of students in a corridor in the Faculty of Education, about to enrol in a teaching degree majoring in English and History, when a professor he'd never seen before walked over to him.

'Show me your enrolment form,' he said kindly.

Eddie showed him what was written on his enrolment form – English and History, the two humanities subjects that Eddie had most loved in high school.

'That's what I want to teach,' Eddie told the Professor, whose name he didn't even know. 'I want to pass on my love of those subjects to my own students one day.'

The Professor studied Eddie closely and said, 'Uh, look, I'm not here to force you to change your mind but, at least at the moment in New South Wales, we actually have *plenty* of English and History teachers. Lots and lots of very good ones.

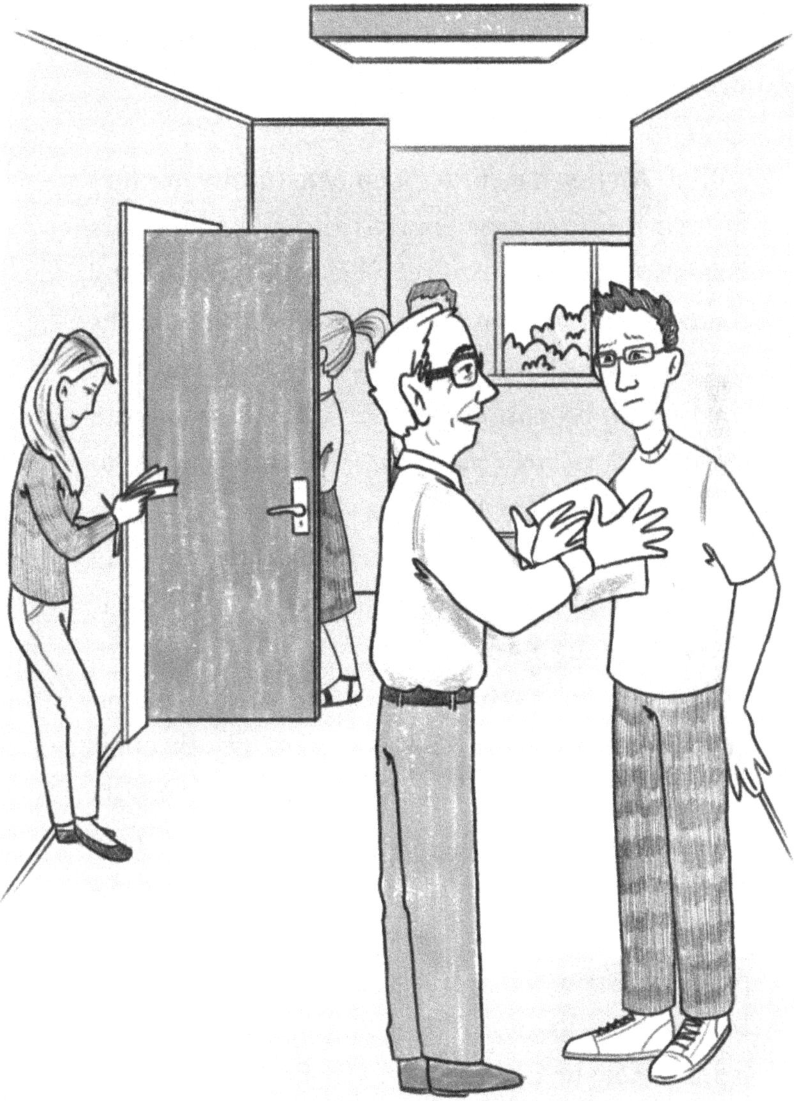

But you know what we don't have? We don't have many Maths teachers. That's where the real, dire need is.'

Maths? Eddie's skin prickled.

'But Maths has never come naturally to me!' he told the Professor. 'Sure, I did a Mathematics Extension 1 subject in Year 12, getting by on my memory and guessing from the cues in the Maths questions which formula I was supposed to use, but the English Extension 2 subject where I got to write stories and poems was my *jam*. Teaching people to love stories the way I love stories, will be my thing. I've never had any deep conceptual understanding of Maths and I just don't really get the *point* of it. It's so dry and unknowable.'

It was true. While Eddie had always had a good memory that could help him get through memorising all the formulae and steps he was supposed to take to reach the right answer, he knew that really great Maths students could use the tools and building blocks of Maths to approach and solve problems creatively by combining those tools and building blocks in different and unexpected ways. Eddie knew he'd never found that experience easy during his time at school.

But when he told the Professor all this, the Professor said, 'Even though you didn't *enjoy* Maths, you do have enough of a foundation to build on and you can pour all of your obvious enthusiasm into teaching kids *the story of maths* instead.'

The Professor added, 'You don't have a *problem* with Maths, young man. You've *persevered* with Maths. You *can* do this.'

'But I want to have a real and personal impact on young people!' Eddie insisted. 'And the best way I can do that is through teaching them English and History.'

The Professor shook his head. 'The real impact you can make is by showing them you care and that they can do what they are setting out to achieve.'

Eddie thought about this for a long time as the queue snaked forward. He'd seen for himself what a lasting and positive impact a good teacher could make. He wanted to do that too. So maybe it didn't really matter what the subject was, so much. If there was an acute need in Mathematics, maybe it *would* make sense for him to become a Maths teacher. The idea had never occurred to Eddie before. Him and *Maths* teaching? It seemed *weird* and *unexpected*.

'Would you consider changing your degree?' the Professor said finally. 'We could really, really use more Maths teachers who are passionate about teaching. Just think about it?'

Then the Professor walked off and Eddie never spoke to him ever again. To this day, Eddie still doesn't know what the Professor's name was.

As the queue kept inching forward, Eddie really thought about his choices for a long time. For Eddie, it really was about working with kids – not about a particular subject. Although Maths had always been a bit of a mystery to Eddie. He'd often wondered over the years, *What is this subject really about? Why are kids forced to learn it for 10 or 11 years? Why does it even matter?* The same way that music was hard and inaccessible to him, but also something that every culture in the world seemed to have invented, Maths seems just as hard and inaccessible but also strangely universal. Music had seemed like a dry, joyless and solitary exercise to Eddie, much like Maths was. But maybe Maths, like music, was a natural part of being human. But it didn't *feel* natural. He was sure that no one *ever* thought about Maths that way, as being *natural.* They either loved it, or they hated it. Eddie wondered if he would have what it took to stand up in front of a class every day and say, 'You should learn this – this really matters. It's part of who you are, you just don't know it yet.'

So Eddie did something that people later thought sounded a little bit crazy or impetuous. He took a pen out of his backpack and changed his major from *English* and *History* to *Maths* and *Technology* instead because the reason he wanted to be a high school teacher in the first place was to help kids like he was once. As a Year 11 prefect, he'd found that transformation – from being a terrified Year 7 to a self-assured Year 11 – amazing to watch, and a huge privilege to be part of. So it wasn't so much the subject, Eddie reasoned with himself – yes, the subject *was* important because you had to like it enough to get it across to people. But what was really at stake here was getting involved in the very personal journey of someone's learning and growth. That was what Eddie truly loved about mentoring, supporting and teaching.

So if schools are desperate for Maths teachers, I'm in, Eddie thought to himself. *I'll do it.*

THE UNIVERSITY OF
SYDNEY
Faculty of Education
Course
English and History
Maths and Technology

It wasn't easy at all suddenly moving from being a Humanities geek to majoring in Maths teaching at university. Eddie often wondered if he'd made the right choice as he thought up ways to make learning Maths less hard. *He* found it hard. How was he going to teach it to kids who might not even be interested?

Eddie's family and his faith, and his friends from high school, kept him going. Four of them ended up at the University of Sydney with him, although they were studying different degrees like Commerce, Engineering and Arts. Believing that he was part of something bigger, that one day he might make a real difference to the children in his classroom, kept Eddie focused.

And then something sort of magical happened. Eddie – who'd always considered himself a Mathematics outsider – started seeing Maths everywhere and in *everything*.

8

Mathematics is a sense

Eddie still had a very strong memory of the long corridor at James Ruse Agricultural High where the annual results of the Australian Mathematics Competition – a national contest demonstrating the importance and relevance of Maths in students' lives – were posted. The names of the students with prizes and distinctions were always pinned at the front of a very, very long line. Eddie's name *never* appeared there – it usually showed up somewhere nearer the end than the start.

But something happened while Eddie was studying Maths at university. He definitely continued to struggle with it and found that a few of his Maths subjects were almost at the edge of what he could comprehend. He spent hours in the university library with a group of friends, all of them discussing and wrestling with some of the more complex problems together. As Eddie started to get a stronger conceptual understanding of Maths – beyond rote learning complex formulae or making an educated guess in a multiple-choice question situation – he discovered that Maths was *more* than just numbers and symbols. It was a world that Eddie wanted to explore and appreciate, and help his future students to do also.

Eddie was tutoring high school students by this stage and he used to tell them that, 'Maths is patterns and shapes and other connections people wouldn't necessarily think of! Picture a river delta,' he would tell them, 'the branches of a sprawling tree, a bolt of lightning. All the shapes look remarkably alike! But why should they have anything in common? And it isn't just things in natural world that do this.

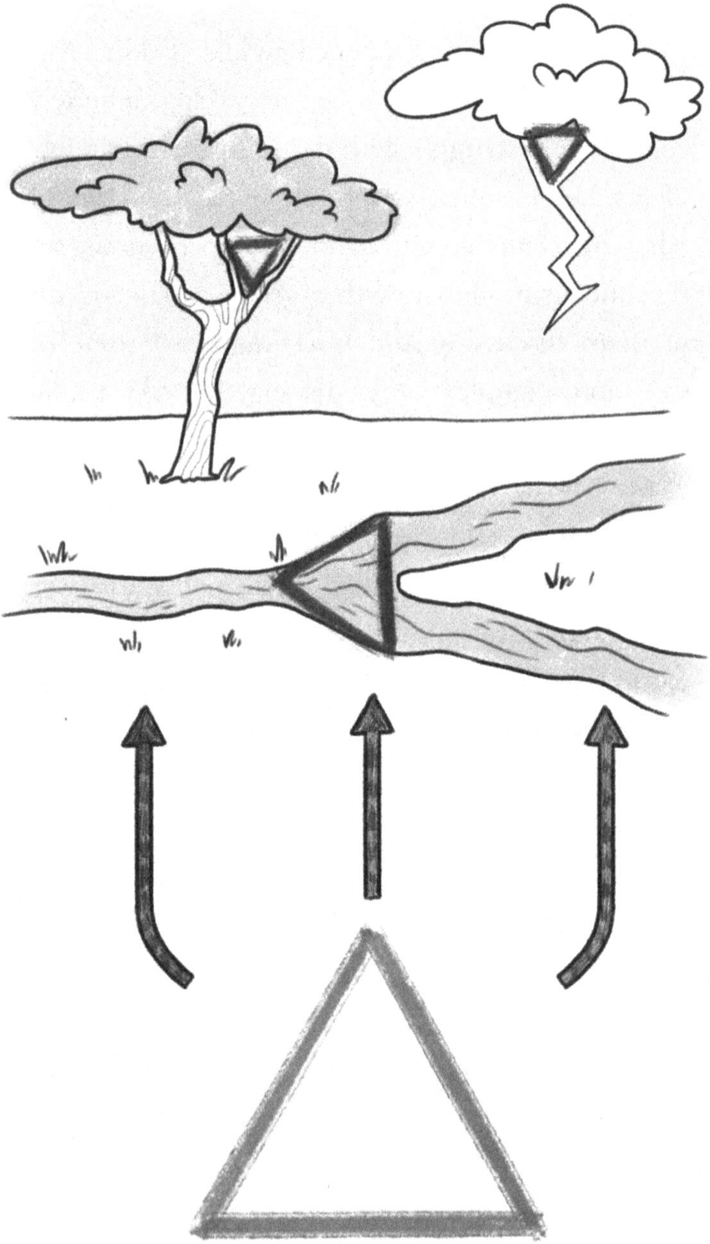

'Look down at the back of your hand,' he would say, 'and study the pattern of blood vessels there that also run throughout your entire body. The human vascular system shares the same characteristics with all of those other things – a central line splitting off into smaller and smaller branches. Every branch is an echo of the greater whole. Every human on earth is filled with these shapes, every cubic centimetre of every body, across the planet. A mathematical reality is actually woven into the fabric of the entire universe. Life on Earth shares similarities with winding rivers, towering trees and raging storms.'

The same way it blew Eddie away once, he could see this amazed his students as well.

'That pattern,' Eddie would tell them, 'is something that Mathematicians call a 'fractal'. Same base as the word 'fraction' or 'fracture'. It means 'broken up into pieces'. Take a good look at nature, at the world, at ancient buildings from human history, at the parts of a flower, how beehives are constructed, the way ice cracks, and you'll see it. Beautiful geometry – shapes and properties – everywhere, and in everything. Somehow, they are all related – they share the same

DNA. Once you have a sense for those patterns, you can't ever *un*see them again.'

> **What are irrational numbers?**
> An irrational number is a number that cannot be expressed as a ratio of two whole numbers. In other words, we can't write it as a simple fraction. Irrational numbers have decimal expansions that go on forever without ever repeating. For example, *Pi* or π, used in the measurement of circles, is an irrational number.

Eddie learned amazing things like this at university every day. He'd never been taught things like this in school, not even at James Ruse. He'd never understood why it was important to learn all those formulae, or even where they had come from. But now, when he looked around at his everyday world, he *could* see the same shapes. A head of broccoli, the leaves of a fern, clouds in the sky, a ball being kicked into a goal. All of them were mathematical because they were made of *patterns*. And he passed on this love of patterns to the students he was tutoring while at university.

He learnt about the special number symbolised by the Greek letter *Pi* or π. It comes from dividing the length around a circle (its circumference) by the length across a circle (its diameter). A simple calculation, but not a simple result: Pi is an 'irrational' number without end that starts off with the familiar numbers 3.14159... but then keeps going with a seemingly random never-ending string of digits. Pi is found all over the natural world: in the cycles of the sun and moon, in the patterns of waves and ripples on the water, even in our DNA! In fact, virtually every aspect of nature is governed by mathematical patterns. For instance, the shells of snails, the petals and florets of flowers, and the leaves and branches of trees all contain structures that follow something called the **Fibonacci sequence**. This is a pattern of numbers that starts with the number 1, then continues by adding the two preceding numbers in the sequence to give you the next one (like 1, 1, 2, 3, 5, 8, 13, 21, 34, 55...).

> **Fibonacci** was an Italian mathematician born around 1170, and died after 1240 who wrote important mathematical texts that are still influential today. At university, Eddie was still learning about some of the things Fibonacci had discovered almost 800 years later!

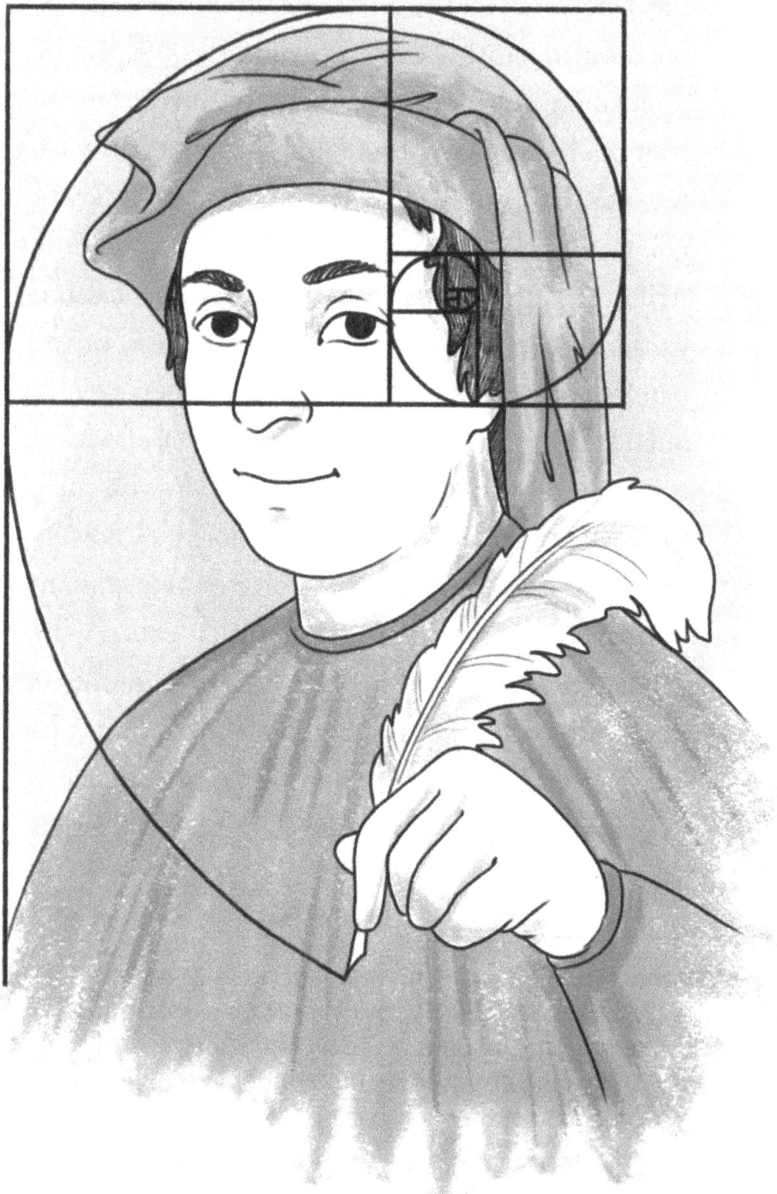

Not only does this sequence appear in many parts of nature, but it has some very unusual characteristics just when you look at it numerically. For instance, if you divide each term by the one before it, you can calculate a series of fractions or ratios. As you go further and further into the Fibonacci sequence, these ratios get closer and closer to another special number, which begins 1.618... (but also goes on forever without repeating – just like Pi). This number is often called the 'golden ratio', 'golden mean' or 'golden section' because it is so aesthetically pleasing to the human eye. For this reason, it has been used by artists, designers and architects down the centuries to make their creations more beautiful! Its symbol is ϕ, which is a Greek letter pronounced *Phi*.

Maths is found everywhere and is for everyone, Eddie thought to himself in wonder.

Sport, cooking, music, carpentry, medicine, astronomy, flying a plane, playing computer games, running a business, Eddie worked out that Maths was at the heart of all of them! No matter what your interests were, or what jobs you wanted to do later in life, it seemed that Maths was integral to them, and understanding Maths would help to do those interests or jobs better, and help people to understand them more deeply.

And even though Eddie would always remember that long corridor of names at James Ruse Agricultural High and how far away from the start of the front he had to walk to find his own name on the list, his new understanding of Maths told him that Maths *was* something natural and *could* be for everyone. He'd discovered that with the right support and attitude, anyone could actually understand the concepts, and master the skills, of Mathematics. And while he'd always gravitated towards those subjects where he had a natural talent or ability, like English or History, Eddie discovered that all it took to understand Maths was time and patience, good problem-solving skills and perseverance.

He still wasn't the fastest at solving problems, or the best at explaining what a formula was for in his Maths tutorial classes at university. But all his years of doing puzzle books meant that Eddie really relished a challenge. He knew that to move on in those puzzle adventures, you *had* to solve a problem.

It was just like life. You couldn't get to the end of the adventure if you weren't patient and didn't keep trying; even when the answer wasn't obvious at all. Eddie had never given up on a single puzzle in his puzzle books when he was a primary school kid, and now he applied the same skills to his university Maths subjects. He never gave up – he tried again and again from different perspectives, he asked lots of questions of his lecturers and friends, and he asked for lots of advice.

Whenever he found that his Maths homework seemed impossible, or way too long, Eddie didn't just walk away, go and watch TV and pretend it wasn't there or even throw his textbooks across the room. He kept trying, he kept asking questions, he kept looking at it from a different angle and then – like magic, although sometimes it took a while to get to the magic – the homework would be done, and he would have gained a deeper understanding of the thinking behind a formula. The problem would be solved. And Eddie would have learnt something new – about the world, about the history of Maths and even about himself and what he was capable of.

Eddie worked out that Maths, like teaching, was about human connection. To really understand something, to not be afraid of something, was to understand what connection it had with your own life. And Maths had everything to do with everyday situations: buying a burger at McDonald's and working out the change? Took Maths. Kicking a ball on a field to get it into the goal (the trajectory of which takes the shape of a parabola, a kind of U-shaped curve)? Took Maths. Managing your money to work out if you could afford that cool shirt or skateboard? Took Maths. Maths was as necessary as breathing. And the fact that every culture in the world had discovered Maths – meant it had to be important. It was worth doing.

Like music – which Eddie started to play more and more after becoming a guitarist in his church band in his late teens and discovering that he'd been surrounded his whole life by a musical ocean that he was only just beginning to dip his toes into – Maths had always been there, but he hadn't been open to it. But now he was.

He began to see that Maths wasn't only immensely practical – it could even be beautiful. It wasn't just about finding answers, but learning to ask the right questions and forming new ways to *see* problems by combining insight with imagination. Mathematics *was* a story just like all the stories Eddie had loved to read, and write, over the years; it had a beginning in every culture in the world and was still developing to this day. It was also history – human history – only not written in words, but in numbers, patterns and formulae.

It gradually began to dawn on Eddie that Mathematics was a *sense*. Just like sight or touch. Understanding Maths let you see things that might otherwise be invisible (like the patterns in nature) and let you build buildings, machines and other things that had never been built before – things like the Sydney Opera House (a structure based on complex mathematical concepts), or the Leaning Tower of Pisa, a bell tower of remarkable symmetry which is located in the very town where Fibonacci the Mathematician was born. Like a sense of rhythm, or a sense of humour, Mathematics, Eddie worked out, was a sense for patterns, relationships and logical connections. It was just a different way to see the world, a way of perceiving things; that's all it was. Maths was like having a superpower – kind of like X-ray vision. Once you understood Maths was just a sense, it changed the way your eyes and mind worked. You saw the world with fresh eyes. Maths had been hidden in plain sight, his entire life. Why had he ever been afraid of it?

The same way he would never say that, because he was short-sighted and had always struggled to see without his glasses, he was not a *seeing kind of person*, Eddie vowed never again to say that Maths wasn't his thing or that he *Couldn't Do Maths*. Any student that ever came to him saying that in future, Eddie knew he would take special care to work with to change that misconception.

He realised that human beings are wired to see patterns because we live in a patterned universe or *cosmos* (Greek for *a well-ordered whole*) not a *chaos* (Greek for *complete disorder and confusion*). It just took the right guidance and teaching for that fear about Maths to fall away, Eddie thought to himself. The same way the fear was falling away for him, he wanted to help others achieve that feeling of *I can* do *this. I can Maths!*

When Eddie was struggling through his university assignments late at night though, he had no idea that, one day, Maths really would become one of the central pillars of his existence. That Maths would take him around the world, even make him famous – possibly the most famous Maths teacher in the world – and help him to reach students in places he'd never been to, or even heard of.

9

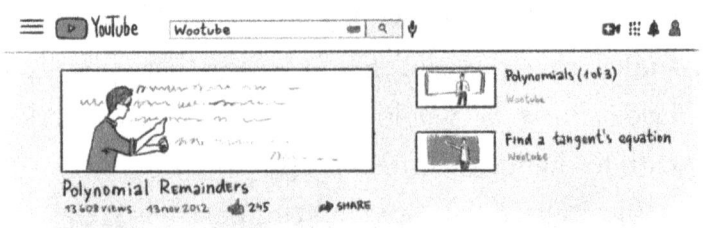

Mister Wootube

After Eddie graduated as a teacher, he taught maths at a few different high schools including his old high school, James Ruse Agricultural High. It felt strange, but also kind of amazing, to be back in the familiar classrooms and halls where he'd spent so many happy hours. Except that he was at the front of the classroom this time and some of his old teachers were now his friends and colleagues! While Eddie worked as a teacher at his old school, all three of his children arrived on the scene – his daughter was born the first year that Eddie was there, his middle son was born a couple of years later and his youngest son was born the year that he transferred to another school.

Eddie has a distinct memory from his first year of teaching at James Ruse High of respectfully disagreeing with one of his old teachers, who was in his fifties at the time.

'Doing all of this administration and paperwork is a waste of time,' the older man had said as they stood by the photocopier together. 'Does any of it even make a difference? There doesn't seem to be much of a point.'

Eddie had replied, 'But there is a purpose, right? We do these things because, ultimately, it helps the kids. That's what it's all about in the end, isn't it?'

'Ah, yes, that's the same mistake we all make,' the other man replied tiredly. 'You *can't* change the lives of children.'

But Eddie secretly disagreed, and he knew it was up to him to maintain his energy and enthusiasm and to not become cynical and worn down by the job. Even then, he understood that the work of a teacher is hard, but it's incredibly important, and teaching *is* capable of making enormous changes in a student's life.

Eddie stayed at his old school as a teacher for a few years, finding that the hardest thing about being a teacher was to show anger and maintain control in his classroom. After everything that Eddie had been through as a kid, he wanted to be a relaxed and laid-back kind of Maths teacher. So, whenever he had to be strict with, or even discipline, a student, he remembered those days when he was sent off to the Principal's office (for things that weren't even his fault) and how terrible that had felt.

In the beginning, Eddie thought that maintaining a safe and cohesive classroom meant that he had to shout and point a lot, but quickly found out most of his students just tuned him out when he did that. And there were always a few who wanted to make Eddie so mad that he *would* shout and point, just so that they could be the centre of attention! Some days he felt like he was living the same day over and over again – he would try to act angry, the students would go quiet for 10 or 15 minutes, then something would happen in class and he'd have to raise his voice again, and on it went. Days like that, Eddie had to remind himself not to feel cynical or worn down, too.

After a while, Eddie worked out that it was better to develop a friendly connection with his students, commanding their respect in the classroom, not by shouting and pointing but by displaying an appropriate level of disapproval and explaining that there were consequences for behaviour that hurt, confused or frightened other people. Even if Eddie didn't actually *feel* angry, he employed his old drama skills from his long-ago Drama subjects to get his students' attention and make them work with each other more co-operatively.

Some of the techniques he used included using the full range of his voice to convey meaning, emphasis and emotion, and using body language to develop a good rapport (or relationship) with his students. Instead of towering over them while he explained something tricky, Eddie would try to kneel or sit beside them to indicate that they were working through the problem *together*. He also use improvisational skills – such as building on or repeating ideas his students raised – that he'd learned from Drama class to build trust so that mistakes could be turned into illuminating examples for the entire class to work through, together, without

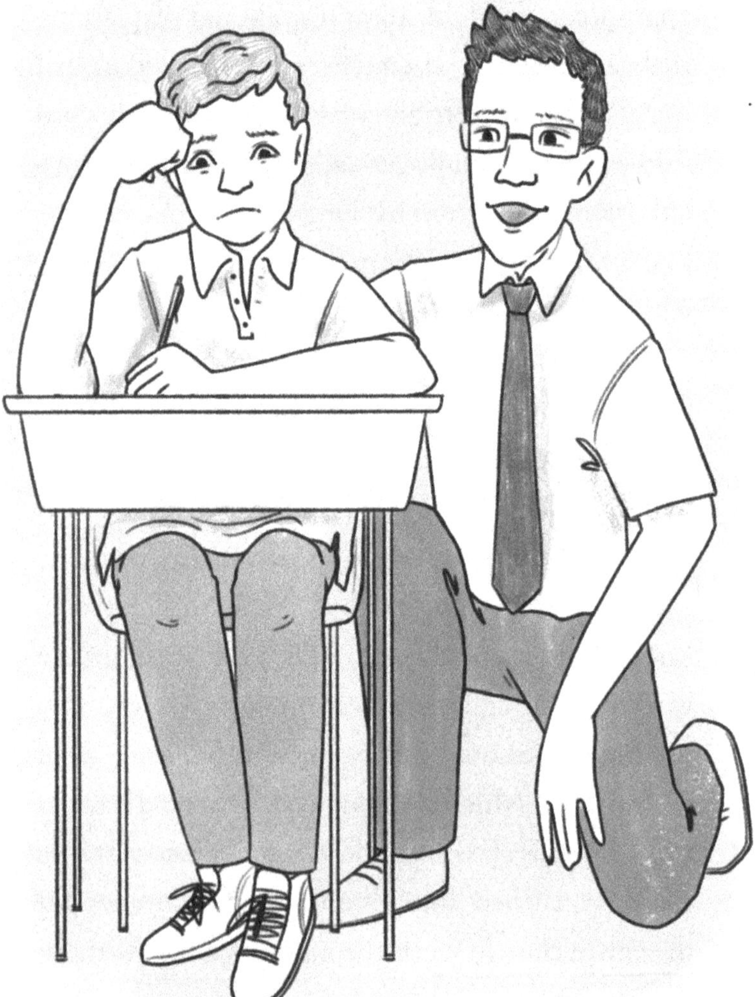

humiliating the person who'd made the mistake in the first place. Eddie would always tell them it was okay to make mistakes because that's how you learned things, through trial and error.

Using his skills from high school as a storyteller and scriptwriter, he designed every single lesson he gave around the classic three-act structure (setup/conflict/resolution) that you might see in a play in a theatre. The 'setup' helped students to understand the foundational knowledge they needed for that class. The 'conflict' stage helped to provide tension and interest through the set problems that were the challenge for the students to solve. And the 'resolution' stage was used to explain to the students why they needed that particular new concept or skill to resolve the problems encountered.

When Eddie was 28 years old and had been teaching at James Ruse for about six years, the opportunity to be Head Maths Teacher came up at Cherrybrook Technology High School, a selective school in The Hills area where he had grown up. Eddie grabbed it. Being Head Maths Teacher would let him *shape* the Maths curriculum (a fancy way of saying the subjects that made up the Maths course and how they were taught) a bit more than he was doing at James Ruse.

But it was a lot harder being the Head of Maths, with a much bigger workload and responsibilities. At the same time, Eddie started to realise that his students really depended on him and the quality of his own work as a teacher – if he took shortcuts or didn't prepare properly, they were the ones who suffered the consequences. If they didn't understand what he wanted them to do, they weren't going to thrive in Maths and they would switch off and fall behind.

The school was the largest selective school in the whole of New South Wales with around 2,000 students from about 60 different cultures, speaking a range of different languages. It was a lot bigger than James Ruse Agricultural High, and with more students came more serious, real-life issues. Students weren't just contending with school – many of them were dealing with really difficult issues at home that might sometimes make them angry, lash out, be unresponsive or even interrupt their learning.

Some students didn't even have enough to eat, or where they were living wasn't physically or emotionally safe. And some were constantly being shuttled between their parents' separate homes or were caring for sick family members or working more than one job just to support the household income, like an adult would. Being at Cherrybrook Technology High School every day really increased Eddie's sense of empathy for others.

Eddie came to realise that a teacher's work was never done. His lessons could always be clearer, more feedback could always be given, or given more quickly, and there would always be students needing more time outside the classroom for one-on-one help and support that wasn't just about Maths.

It broke his heart every time he realised that a student might need much more from him than just academic support. As he and his fellow teachers learned which students didn't have a safe or happy home environment, they would step up and offer them more support and guidance because school was probably the safest, most stable thing in their lives.

So Eddie's new job was both immensely rewarding but also intensely heartbreaking – there would always be more that he could do to help his students and he wished, every day, that he could do more, and that there were more hours in the day to do them in.

Then in 2012, Eddie began to notice a very familiar pattern emerging in his classroom.

One of Eddie's 16-year-old Year 10 students started to lose weight and to skip classes – not because he wasn't a good student, but because he was very, very ill. Eddie soon found out that the student had been diagnosed with pancreatic cancer, a part of the body that secretes enzymes which help you to digest food. It was a tricky cancer to treat, with a very low survival rate, and the boy started to be away from school for huge chunks of time; getting the sorts of serious treatment that Eddie's own mother had gone through, years before.

Eddie remembered how many of his later years in high school had been deeply affected by his mum's cancer, and what that had done to his marks, and to his education. Eddie wasn't quite sure how he could help this student but he felt, deep down, that he needed to do *something* to stop his student falling further and further behind.

The student would have to miss weeks and weeks of school for chemotherapy and radiotherapy. Eddie thought it wouldn't be right for the boy to be struggling away alone at home with just his textbook; especially as he would be feeling sick and exhausted from all the treatment. How could Eddie actually walk through all the ideas with this student the same way he was doing with all his other students in class? Eddie wondered. He wanted to help the boy understand the concepts straight from Eddie himself, and not just from a dry textbook, on his own.

Unlike the days where Eddie had slept through class and there was no way to play back what the teacher had said while he was sleeping, Eddie realised that we now have the technology to help people learn, even if they can't be in the classroom, in person.

He thought to himself, *Why don't I just take my phone and when the lesson starts, I'll hit* record?

Eddie had no idea how to prop his phone up at the right height, so one lunchtime, he went down to the woodworking room and made himself a weird-looking tripod out of wood that the phone could sit on. Then he used that to start recording every Year 10 Maths lesson he taught.

After he'd recorded each lesson, Eddie posted it online. Then he sent the link to his student and the student's family at the hospital, letting them know that the video of that lesson was on YouTube, just for him, and free for him to use.

All of Eddie's other students started to notice what he was doing because Eddie wouldn't start his class until he'd set up the clunky little homemade, wooden contraption on a table first before placing his phone on it and hitting *record*. He only ever filmed himself talking, not the other students. But whenever one of the other kids yelled out a question or had an *A-ha! moment*, as Eddie liked to call those moments where someone suddenly grasped a mathematical concept they'd been struggling with, the video would pick all that up and the boy would hear all his friends and classmates yelling out in the background. Eddie hoped that that would make him feel as if he was right there with them all, learning.

'Hey, what's that about, sir?' one of the boys asked one day, pointing at the clunky wooden stand with Eddie's phone balanced on top of it.

When Eddie explained, the boy laughed and said, 'Not YouTube, sir, *Woo*tube!'

And sure enough, Eddie's own students started to watch 'Wootube', and they started passing the links to the videos to their friends in other classes, and then those students started to pass them on to friends from other schools. It helped that you could watch things back that hadn't made sense at the time because Eddie did talk a little bit too fast! You could even slow Eddie's voice down or speed it up so that you could skip the parts that already made sense and get to the parts of the lesson that didn't.

Eddie didn't realise the snowball effect that his Maths videos were having. He thought he was teaching and supporting *one* student who was going through a really, really tough time. But kids he wasn't even teaching were starting to use Wootube to look up Maths topics they didn't understand, not just in Sydney, but in small outback towns like Cobar in rural New South Wales.

The fact that the videos were free to anyone to use made them uniquely equalising and inclusive. Students and teachers who were isolated didn't need to travel anywhere or pay anything to watch them. Students loved his videos because you could replay, skip through or pause them as often as you needed to when you were studying for a test.

Teachers, especially at small, isolated, rural schools, also loved them, because it was almost as if Eddie could stand in for them as an 'extra' teacher. If the students there weren't listening to their classroom teacher or needed extra help, Eddie could 'be there' – to explain things again. Having Maths taught to you by someone different, the teachers found, often made their students sit up and really take notice.

At the time when Eddie posted his first Wootube video for his seriously ill student, little did he know that he would one day have over *one million* subscribers to his Wootube video channel or that his videos would be seen by students, parents and teachers around the world more than *71 million times*!

What Eddie had been trying to do, with those original videos, was to tell his student that *We are going to learn this, together.* He had no way of knowing, when he first pressed *record* where being 'Mister Wootube' was going to lead.

10

Where empathy gets you

By 2015, Eddie had set up a second YouTube channel, called Wootube^2 (Wootube squared!), to help people who were interested in *teaching* mathematics. He was amazed to have hit almost 10,000 subscribers on his original Wootube channel for students and, by then, his videos had had almost one million views from people living in 223 countries! Some of which Eddie knew that he'd probably never even get to visit in his lifetime.

Being a Technology teacher now at Cherrybrook Technology High School, as well as Head of Maths, he'd upgraded from using his old phone to make his lesson videos and was now using a brand-new iPad on a proper tripod to record each topic instead. His students were completely used to it by now and didn't bat an eyelash when they came into the classroom and saw the iPad and tripod ready to go.

Eddie still didn't ask people to pay a single cent to watch his videos because he continued to believe that education should be *free*, and accessible to everyone. And the good news was, the sick student that had started Eddie down this interesting road had graduated from school and had gained a place at university after recovering from his treatment. It had all definitely been worth it. Eddie had just set out to help *one* person – and now he was helping thousands, possibly even ... millions?

What had started out as a YouTube channel covering specific topics for a specific student had become something much broader by then, and Eddie now found himself recording every lesson that he ran for his own students and also extra videos for students from Year 7 through to Year 12.

He'd even started to cover extension Maths topics for kids who needed even more Maths, and all because he liked using technology to help kids learn Maths on their own terms, and in their own time.

His days were now really busy – when he wasn't teaching, filming in class, talking to other teachers or editing his videos for uploading to Wootube or Wootube², he was helping his wife, who worked as an accountant, look after their three young children. Eddie's children often needed to go to the doctor, or be rushed to the hospital, because they'd had a bad allergic reaction or asthma attack. Eddie was always patient with them because he knew himself how bad allergies and asthma could be. He wasn't covered from head to toe in Vaseline or Band-Aids anymore, but he still remembered the feeling of badly wanting to scratch, and all the things he wanted to eat but couldn't because he was allergic to them.

Then in 2015, Eddie was nominated for, and won, the *New South Wales Premier's Prize for Innovation in Science and Mathematics Education* that year, a prize from the State Government in recognition of all the hard work he was doing inside and outside the classroom to bring the joy of learning Maths to people in the State where he lived, and beyond. Eddie was stunned because he was doing what he always did – trying to make a positive impact on his students' lives and being there to support them in their school career and to help them grow. And he did this in interesting and novel ways that included teaching them card tricks and getting them to flip bottles of half-drunk water multiple times out in the schoolyard, just to demonstrate how probability worked, and that Maths could be found in places that you least expected.

Eddie had found over the years that he'd made the greatest impact when he'd had the courage to follow his convictions, and teach and do things *his* way, rather than just listening to the opinions of others. Courage and belief had led him to becoming a teacher in the first place when others, even some of his high school teachers and his own mum and dad, had told him teaching was a waste of his skills and opportunities. Courage and belief had led him to start recording and posting his lessons online when others said it would be too hard. Courage and belief had pushed him to become a leader in education when other people told him he was too young and inexperienced.

Although his mum never got to see the kind of teacher Eddie had become, he often heard his mum's wise words from the past in his head as he struggled to make the right choices every day. He liked to think that she'd be proud of him and how far he had come.

*

That first award was followed in 2016 by a *ChooseMATHS Teacher Excellence Award* from the Australian Mathematical Sciences Institute

(AMSI) for a scheme that Eddie had come up with for struggling Year 7 and 8 Maths students at Cherrybrook Technology High School. Eddie called it 'MathsPASS' (Peer-Assisted Study Sessions). It linked these students to Year 11 students who could help them study Maths and build skills and confidence, not just in Maths, but in life.

One of the things Eddie still loved about teaching Maths was seeing the joy and thrill of the *A-ha! moment* in his classroom – when a student's eyes widened, they literally gasped in shock and leant back in their chair, clasping their head as if their brain had just exploded because something had suddenly made complete sense! Getting to experience lots of *A-ha! moments* with his students meant that getting awards for it were just the icing on the cake. Although Eddie couldn't see all the *A-ha! moments* happening in places as far away as New Zealand, Africa or Greenland (where people were watching his Maths videos around the clock, 365 days a year!) he felt good knowing that maybe they were, and that he was helping with that.

That AMSI award was soon followed by an Alumni Award from his old university, the

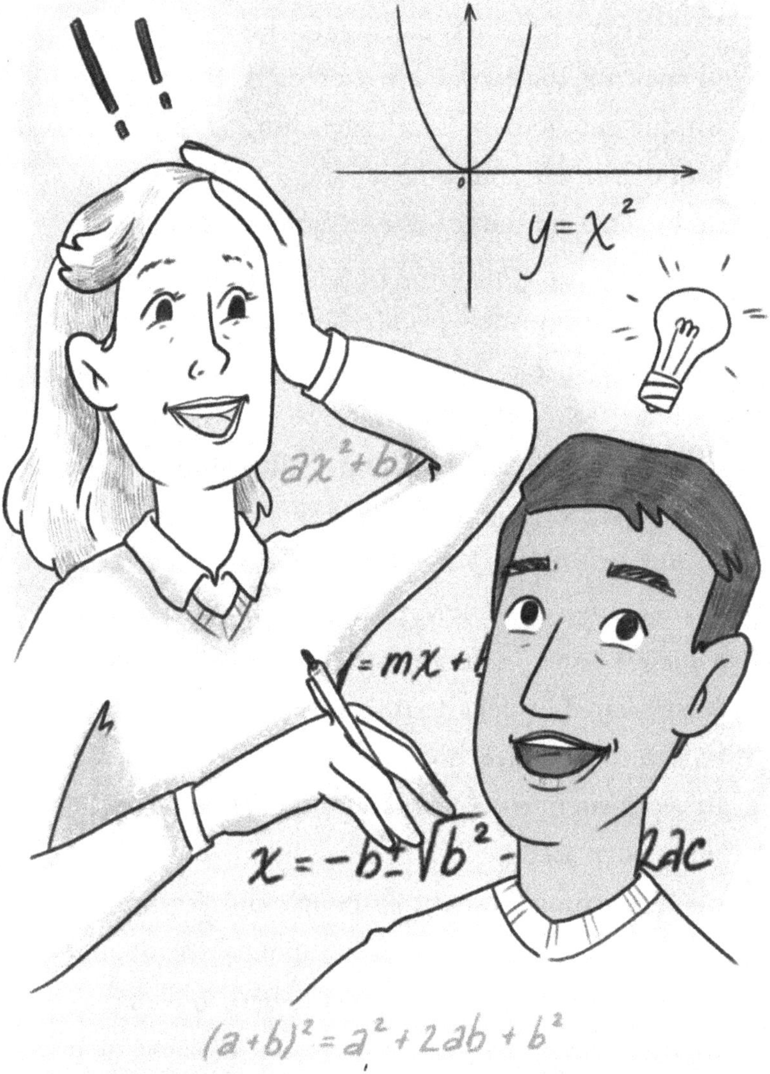
$y = x^2$
$(a+b)^2 = a^2 + 2ab + b^2$

University of Sydney, in 2017, for his contribution to making the world a better place through his unique methods of Maths teaching. Eddie soon found himself standing on stage with a famous architect, a computer science pioneer, an orchestra conductor, a well-known scientist and lots of other distinguished people he never would have otherwise met.

That year, the Commonwealth Bank also awarded Eddie a Teaching Fellowship for his MathsPASS program and for his work as a volunteer with the University of Sydney's *Widening Participation and Outreach* program which helped regional and remote students living across Australia. The fact that Eddie had gone to an agricultural high school also meant that whenever he went out into rural and remote communities, he often surprised people because he knew so much about farming. Sometimes people didn't think he *looked* as if he knew anything about farming, but Eddie would manage to surprise them and change their expectations and assumptions all over again when he started talking about beef production, or crop rotation.

All of these awards and experiences had sprung from a simple idea – to help a student in need to learn without barriers. In 2018, that simple idea took Eddie even further than the primary school kid he used to be could ever imagine.

11

Be a mathematician

If Eddie had to name one of the most amazing years of his life so far, surely 2018 would be among them.

He was asked to give the Australia Day Address for that year, a speech where someone *famous* in Australian life (Eddie couldn't even believe that part of it when he was asked!) traditionally reflects on Australia's identity and the diversity of its society. Eddie was asked to share his experiences as an Australian, and his thoughts about our history.

This was a brilliant opportunity for Eddie to talk about the amazing job that teachers do and ask that people value our schools and teachers a lot more than they do.

Eddie also shared with the whole of our country how, when he was little, he was treated badly for not being 'Australian' (even though he was) because to the kids who used to bully him, he didn't look 'Australian.' For a long time, Eddie told his audience, he had grown up thinking that 'Australians' were other people, and it took him years, and a lot of kindness and care from his friends and teachers at James Ruse Agricultural High, to realise that he actually was Australian and that being Australian has fundamentally shaped him as a person, and as a teacher.

Eddie also talked about how teaching was a great source of joy for him, but also of moral purpose, because education is a powerful weapon that can change the world. Education allows people to appreciate the things that bring us together as human beings, but also to celebrate and honour all our differences, too.

'It is through learning Mathematics,' Eddie told the crowd of important people gathered at the Sydney Conservatorium of Music that day or watching via the Internet at home or on their mobile devices, 'that each student can become a different person and that their character can grow. They learn to persevere through difficulty when an answer isn't obvious. They develop clarity of thought and the ability to argue logically. They learn the ability to deal with complexity. And most importantly, they learn to see things from different perspectives. Every time we take a new perspective – we learn something new.'

Eddie invited everyone listening *to be a mathematician* because, he said, 'Mathematics can make us all *more* human. Mathematicians learn to see things from a different perspective and when you do that with a fellow human being – that's called *empathy*. If you do that with your local community – by looking at the social patterns around you – you might be able to change them for the better. Maths is about looking at lots of different things, like people who might look, sound or believe differently, and calling them all by the same name: *Australians*, while also acknowledging the sovereignty of our First Nations peoples, past and present, and their stewardship of this beautiful country that we call home.'

Eddie also urged his listeners to see a need and to follow it, the same way he did when he started filming his classes for his sick student in 2012.

'Fulfilment,' Eddie reminded his listeners, 'isn't found in looking into yourself, it's found in looking to others and having a heart to serve them with the gifts that you've been given. One of the things I love best about teaching is that *every child is gifted*. I really believe that. I get the joy of discovering *how* they're gifted, and helping them to learn to use their gifts.'

Finally, Eddie reminded his audience that, 'Everyone has a story, and everyone's story is worth learning from. In my story, being a teacher is how I learned that regardless of who they are or where they live, all children can flourish in this ever-changing world if they receive a great education.'

But 2018 wasn't done with Eddie yet! He was soon named the 2018 'Australia's Local Hero' for New South Wales, joining seven other amazing 'local heroes' from around Australia who made things, or did things, to make their communities,

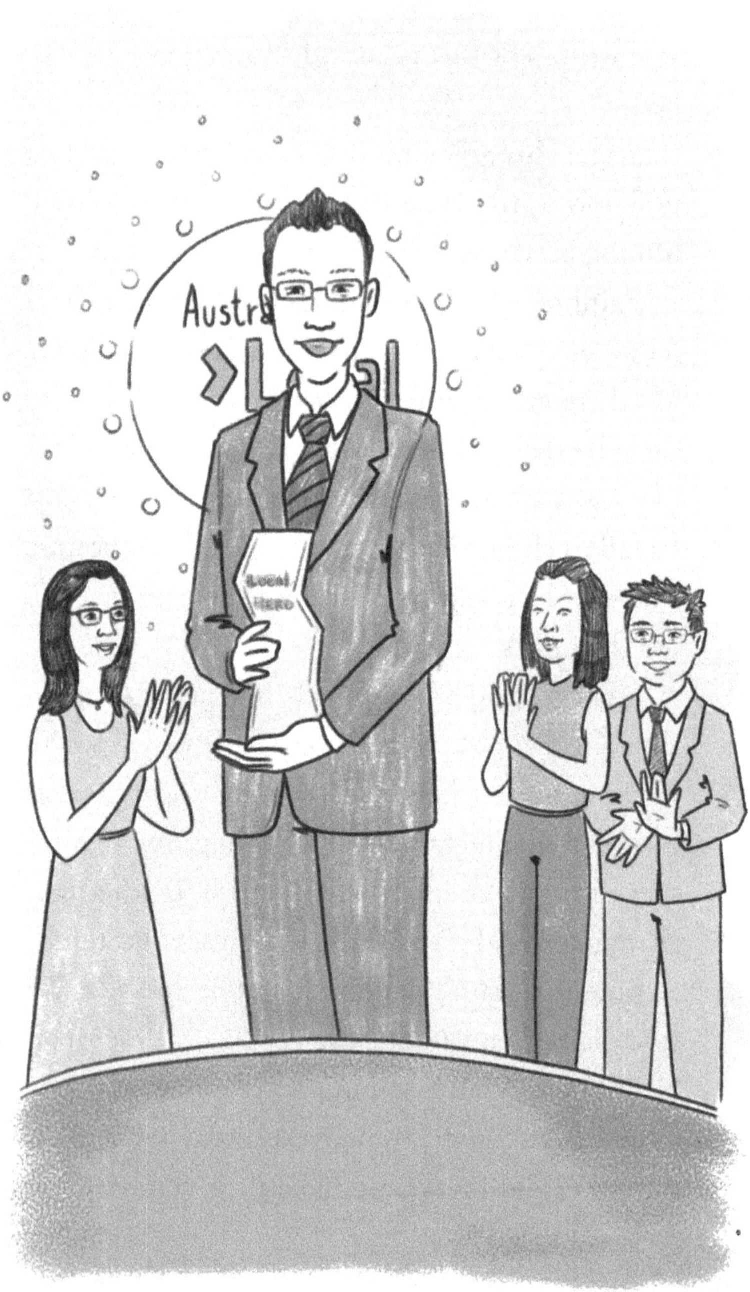

and the world around them, a better place because of their actions. At a ceremony presided over by the Prime Minister of the time, Malcolm Turnbull, which Eddie attended with his proud wife, Michelle, big sister, Kylie, and big brother, Kevin, Eddie heard the Prime Minister name him the whole of Australia's 'Local Hero' for 2018! If you asked Eddie now, he would tell you that he doesn't really remember how he got up there on the huge stage (he might have walked, maybe he floated?), but the Prime Minister brought him back down to earth by shaking his hand firmly and giving him a 'handsome award' (to use the Prime Minister's own words!).

Eddie was really shocked because he'd never expected to win. All those years he'd been told he wasn't 'Australian' by the bullies had meant that when he was told he was the *whole* of Australia's local hero, it didn't make any sense in his brain at all. Eddie would describe the moment his name came out of the Prime Minister's mouth as maybe the same feeling you might have if the people you'd always known as your parents told you suddenly that you were actually adopted! Eddie found it such a strange and wondrous thing to happen. He felt a little bit like an impostor. Every day that Eddie stood in the classroom and taught Maths, he *never* felt like an impostor. But the moment he was about to receive an award for being 'Australian', Eddie did feel a little bit like maybe people had made a mistake in giving him this award, because he'd been told for so long that he wasn't one of us.

As he stood at the podium, Eddie thanked everyone he could think of, especially teachers all around the country, who know the power of giving children the priceless gift of education.

'Education can radically change the trajectory of a child's life,' Eddie told the listening crowd. 'It can transform the possibilities of what a child can become and achieve – changing a life, a family and a community, forever.'

Eddie knew that what he was saying was the truth because it had happened in his own life. He was proof of that.

Hundreds of people in the room listened intently to Eddie's words and his belief that Mathematics was for everyone.

'It's like a magic key that will help you to unlock a beautiful universe of patterns, practical solutions and surprising connections,' Eddie told them.

Like all of Eddie's own videos, his speech from that night can still be seen on YouTube today, as can Eddie's Australia Day Address from 2018.

*

But even more was in store. Later in the year, Eddie won a 'Gold Harold' award for his work with over 1,400 students from disadvantaged backgrounds and was also named as one of the Top 10 teachers *in the entire world* in the Global Teacher Prize from out of more than 30,000 teachers from 173 countries. Eddie was amazed to find a YouTube video of Bill Gates, the legendary co-founder of Microsoft, reading out Eddie's name as one of the Top 10 on the shortlist for the Prize! (That's on YouTube, too).

Being shortlisted from so many teachers around the globe meant that Eddie had to get a new passport – because he'd hardly ever left New South Wales his whole life, and his old one had long since expired. Then he had to leave his wife and three children to fly to Dubai (a country in the United

Arab Emirates in the Middle East) to find out if he had won.

Standing up on stage with nine other amazing teacher finalists from South Africa, the United Kingdom, Brazil, the United States, Belgium, Colombia, Turkey, Norway and the Philippines, Eddie couldn't believe how far he'd come and how much his life had changed, but also not really changed, all at the same time.

If, on that day long ago where he'd told his parents he'd wanted to be a teacher, someone had leant over and said, 'It's going to take you to the

Middle East and put you in the running for a Prize with prize money of one million dollars attached to it!', Eddie would never have believed it for a second. Now, standing on that stage, Eddie felt as if he was still the same teacher, and the same Eddie, underneath. He taught his classes the same way, with the same passion and energy. So, to be recognised for the things he was doing, all the way over in Australia, everyday things ... seemed like a dream.

But as the golden confetti rained down from the ceiling when the winner – inspirational art teacher Andria Zafirakou from the Alperton Community School in London – was announced to a packed and screaming audience, Eddie had to pinch himself. There was shouting, yelling and tears and even a famous comedian on the stage! Eddie was the first to jump to his feet, on stage, to run and give Andria a huge hug to say *Congratulations!* The room was filled with the sound of people raising the roof for teachers and teaching. Eddie didn't think he'd ever be in a situation like this one ever again.

But 2018 had even more in store for Eddie. He became a Mathematics curriculum leader for the

New South Wales Department of Education and an Education Ambassador for the University of Sydney, his old university. It meant that Eddie could help to shape the way that Maths was taught in schools across New South Wales and how teachers were trained at the university. The small boy who used to hide from his primary school teachers was now leading a team of crack teachers and other professionals who were teaching other teachers better, more innovative, tech-smart and more connected ways to teach.

Eddie also became a published author with his first book, *Woo's Wonderful World of Maths* (which was published in Australia, New Zealand and the United States!), soon followed by two of his own Maths activity books, *Eddie Woo's Magical Maths* and *Eddie Woo's Magical Maths 2*. He even started hosting a TV show on the ABC called *Teenage Boss*, which follows teenagers from across Australia who take charge of their family's budget. It's now into its second series.

In 2019 and beyond, Eddie received more awards for the work he was doing and his website continues to fill up with Awards, Maths lesson videos and other amazing projects that Eddie is working on.

Some of these include writing, producing and presenting a video series with the Sydney Opera House about how Mathematics is an integral part of its design; narrating the audio guide for the National Gallery of Victoria's art exhibition *Escher x nendo: Between Two Worlds* which placed the mathematically-precise works of legendary Dutch artist M. C. Escher into 'conversation' with the work of acclaimed Japanese design studio nendo. This led Eddie to become a trustee of the Museum of Applied Arts and Sciences in Sydney.

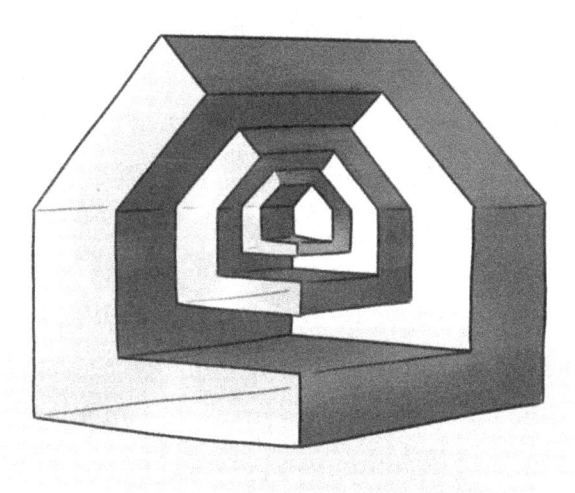

Life was full to overflowing with amazing moments and intense challenges, but Eddie's work also took him away from his classroom and his family a lot more than it used to. Some days he might find himself jumping on a plane just after sunrise to speak to hundreds of school students and teachers in country New South Wales; or in the middle of a serious government advisory meeting about the State or national Maths curriculum.

But the one thing that kept Eddie grounded through the whirlwind of life was to remember that at the heart of everything were his students – whether they were right in front of him in the same classroom, or sitting in a room in Greenland or Brazil. Many of Eddie's own students have caught the fire of learning and teaching Maths from Eddie, the same way Eddie did when he reached university, and have themselves become teachers now. Every time one of Eddie's students becomes a teacher, he reckons it feels like how a proud Granddad would feel.

Eddie's life now, more than ever, is an incredible juggling act, including supporting the learning of so many, like his own children, through difficult circumstances like the COVID-19 lockdowns that swept the country throughout 2020 and into 2021. But the thing Eddie likes to remember in tough times, and incredible times, is that teachers are teaching every hour of the day, not just when they're sitting at the front of a classroom. Teachers are there to help their students interpret and navigate the world around them, and to help students understand what they should value, why learning matters and why *they* matter.

'We change and grow and develop as human beings not on the sunny days, it's on the dark days, that we are confronted with who we are,' Eddie has said. 'What I went through when I was younger gave me a real sense of understanding for what the children I teach go through. I know that in my classroom of 30 kids, I can guarantee there will be three, four or five of them going through the hardest period of their life and *no one knows about it. I* don't know about it, their friends don't know about it. I walk through the playground and look across the faces in a school of 2,000 kids and there must be hundreds of these children going through an enormously difficult time. What they need is just someone to be beside them. So that's enormously shaped the educator, the parent and the person that I am today.'

What Eddie tries to get his students to understand is that they should never close themselves off from subjects like Maths or Science just because they have this idea that they *can't do it*, or *it's too hard*. Whenever a student tells Eddie, 'I can't do Maths, sir!' he makes it his special mission to positively change their thinking because he used to think the same way himself. If Eddie himself had stayed closed off to Maths, his entire adult life as a teacher, and his entire life, would have been totally different.

Eddie's career marries together all of his passions for writing, communication and storytelling with the teaching of STEM subjects. Eddie's own early resistance to Maths shows that no one should ever close themselves off from Maths or other STEM subjects because creativity and storytelling are as inherent in Science, Technology, Engineering and Maths subjects as they are in any other human pursuit. Maths can be found in the most surprising places and things, and Eddie's own story demonstrates the mind-boggling and wonderful places that Maths can lead you to.

Eddie keeps a card in his desk that he received once from one of his former students. She went through a really tough time in her final years of school and often felt very alone, just like Eddie once did when his mother was ill with cancer. Like his teachers at James Ruse Agricultural High, Eddie noticed how unhappy she was and asked if she was all right, one day after class. It was like a dam wall breaking. Things outside school were really tough, she told him. She felt as if she couldn't survive long enough to make it through school to graduate Year 12! So, for the rest of her school days at Cherrybrook, Eddie tried to give that student as much emotional and academic support as he could, by coaching her and checking in with her and by talking with her.

The card Eddie has always kept says:

Your unconditional support has given me confidence in myself, ability and potential. When you spoke about your own personal experiences, I gained a strong sense of hope and belief that I can one day be successful, just like you. Your guidance has completely changed my view of the world, and of my life.

*

Eddie gets emotional whenever he reads this card. It means a lot to him.

If you ask him why, he'll tell you, 'It's an enormous privilege to be given the opportunity to make this kind of impact on a young person, an impact that could really shape them for the rest of their life. I never forget, in every interaction I have with young people now, that my words and actions might impact them the same way that that Professor's words once impacted me.

I can never repay the kindness, time and knowledge that all these people poured into me to help shape the person I've become. But I can pass that gift and that impact on to others. It's also hard knowing that this is what's at stake in our work. The best thing about teaching is that it matters – the hardest thing is that it matters *every single day*.'

Eddie, just like everybody else in the world, was forced to stay home and slow down a lot by the events of 2020 and 2021 when a pandemic – caused

Your unconditional
support has given me
in myself
and potential.
you spoke about
own personal
experiences, I gained a
strong sense of hope
and belief that I can one
day be successful, just
like you. Your guidance
has completely changed my
view of the world,
and of my life.

by the COVID-19 virus – swept across most of the world. Of course, Eddie was well set-up to run his classes and teaching programs remotely – keeping in touch with his students and other teachers through his computer and via other mobile devices.

But the most challenging thing he found about that period was being a teacher to his own three children when they were forced by lockdowns to do all their schooling from home! They wouldn't sit still, they always wanted snacks and they wanted to run around and play outside rather than sit in front a computer, trying to study and do their homework. It took all of Eddie's skills to keep the learning experience a happy one for them, and for his students; whether they were locked down in New South Wales, or beyond.

If you ask Eddie whether he thinks of himself as the world's greatest mathematician or Maths teacher he would say *No*. He can think of many people who are faster and more brilliant at the subject. But Eddie's contribution to teaching is that he's good at breaking down complex ideas in ways that people can understand. Eddie's gift is that he can open up his students' eyes, even the reluctant ones, to the possibilities of learning mind-expanding subjects like Maths, Science, Technology or Engineering.

As the world slowly opens up again, Eddie is busily planning to work with educators, government agencies, universities, book publishers, filmmakers and others around the world to improve education outcomes and change the ways that we perceive and teach Maths. He's a lifelong, card-carrying Maths teacher – so his work will never be done. And everyone who comes into contact with Eddie Woo gets to take away a little spark of joy about Maths; the learning of which can really make life, and the world, better.

Eddie's beautiful universe of patterns and connections

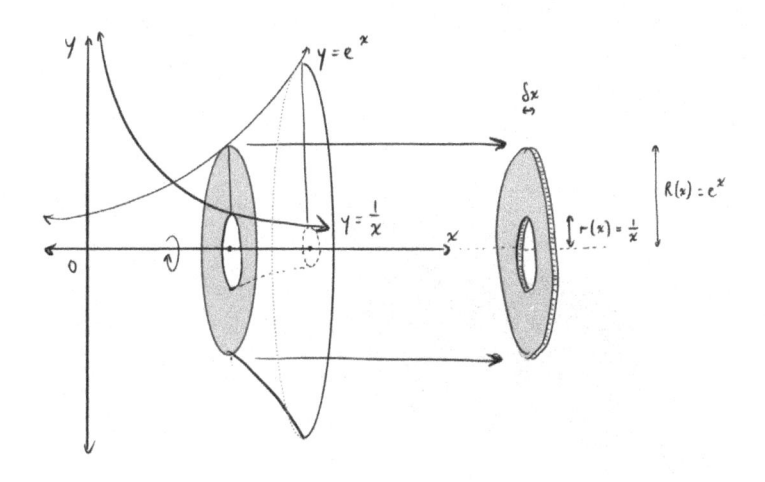

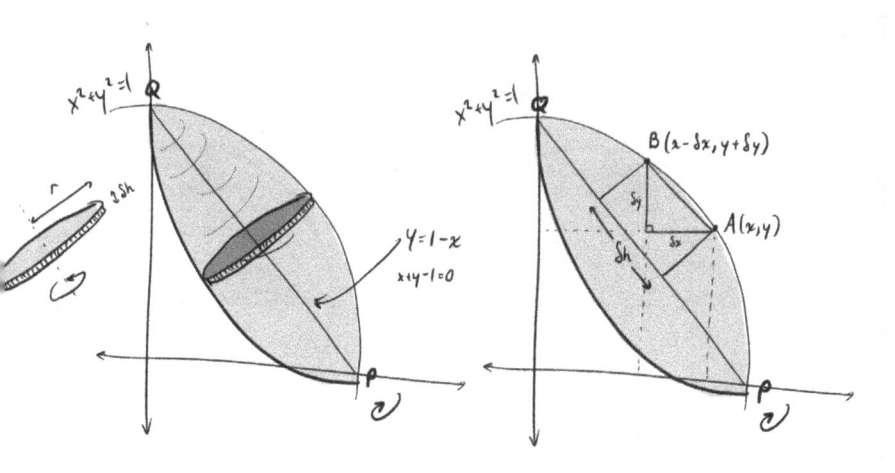

©2021 Eddie Woo

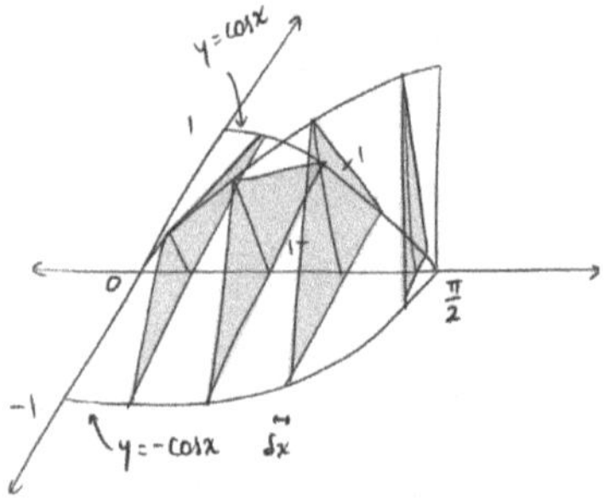
y = cos x
1
1
1
0
π/2
-1
y = -cos x
δx

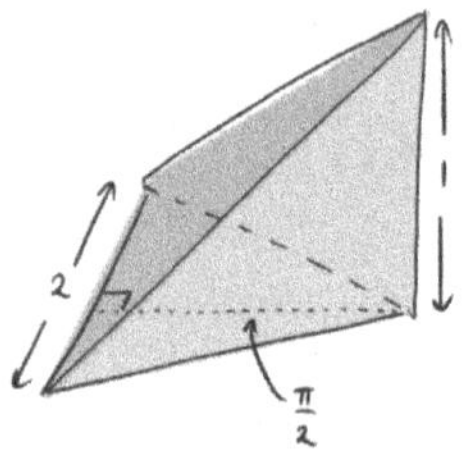
2
1
π/2

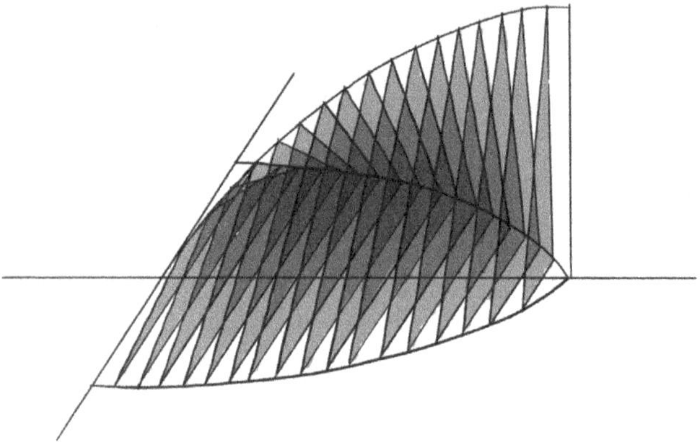

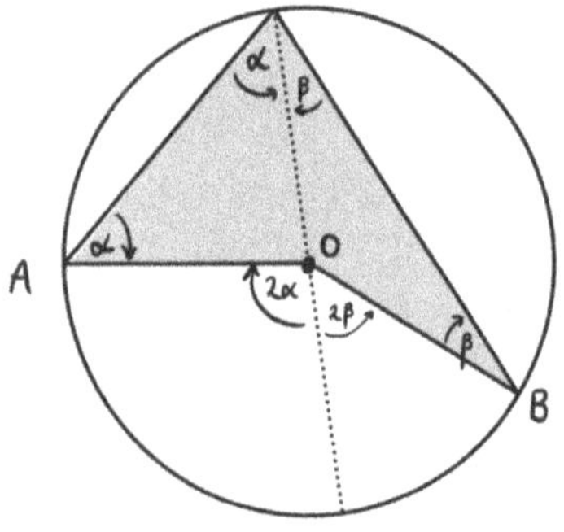
α
β
α
A
O
2α
2β
β
B

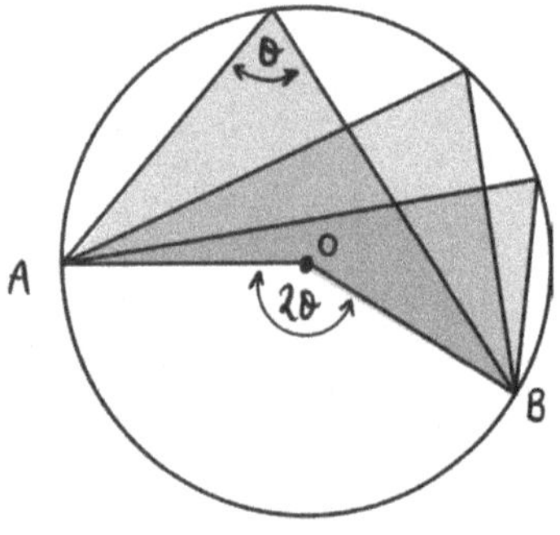
θ
A
O
2θ
B

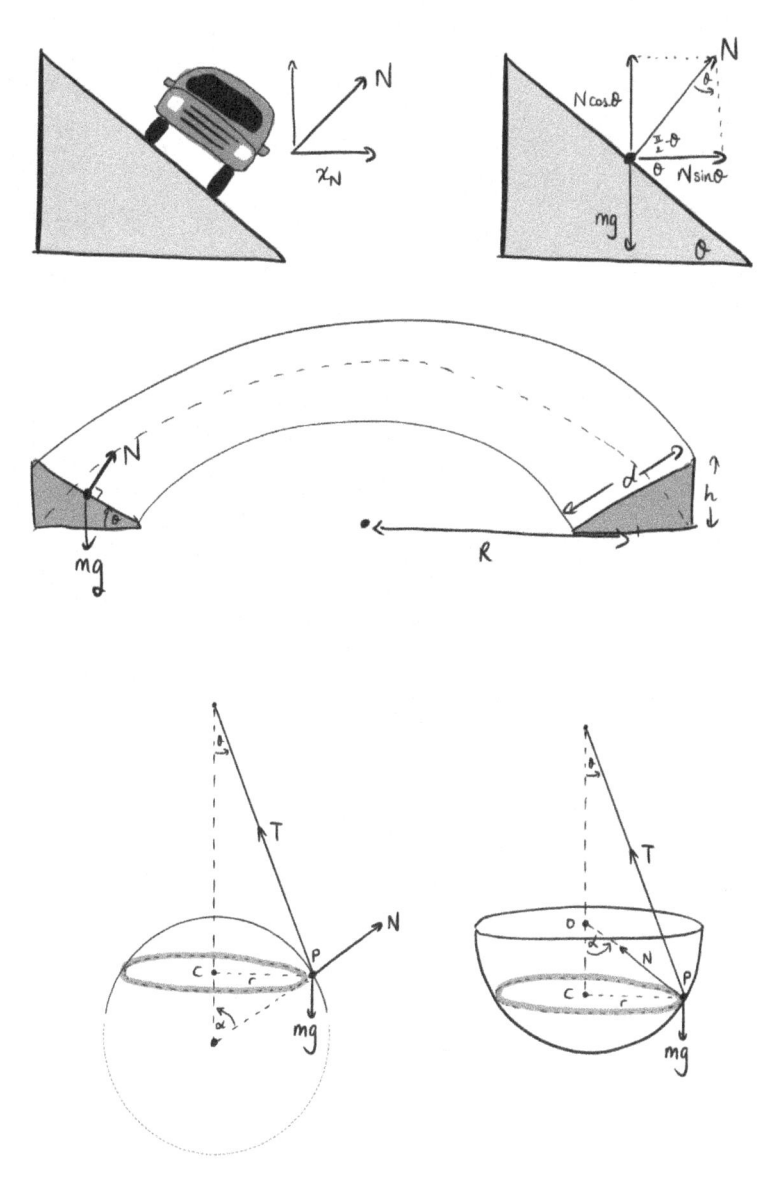

©2021 Eddie Woo

151

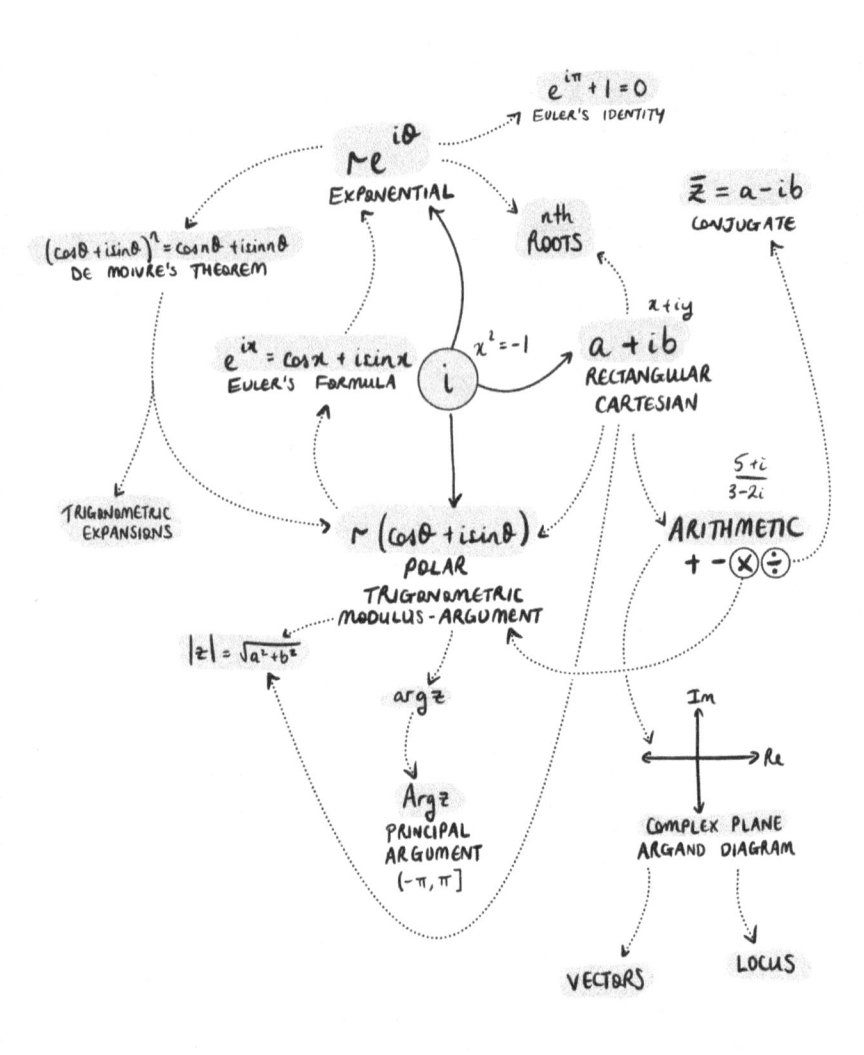

Complex Numbers Mind Map

- $re^{i\theta}$ — **EXPONENTIAL**
  - $e^{i\pi} + 1 = 0$ — EULER'S IDENTITY
  - nth **ROOTS**
  - $(\cos\theta + i\sin\theta)^n = \cos n\theta + i\sin n\theta$ — DE MOIVRE'S THEOREM
    - TRIGONOMETRIC EXPANSIONS

- i (with $x^2 = -1$)
  - $e^{ix} = \cos x + i\sin x$ — EULER'S FORMULA
  - $a + ib$ ($x + iy$) — **RECTANGULAR / CARTESIAN**
    - $\bar{z} = a - ib$ — CONJUGATE
    - $\dfrac{5+i}{3-2i}$ — **ARITHMETIC** $+ - \otimes \div$
  - $r(\cos\theta + i\sin\theta)$ — **POLAR / TRIGONOMETRIC / MODULUS-ARGUMENT**
    - $|z| = \sqrt{a^2 + b^2}$
    - $\arg z$
      - $\mathrm{Arg}\, z$ — PRINCIPAL ARGUMENT $(-\pi, \pi]$

- COMPLEX PLANE / ARGAND DIAGRAM (Im, Re axes)
  - VECTORS
  - LOCUS

©2021 Eddie Woo

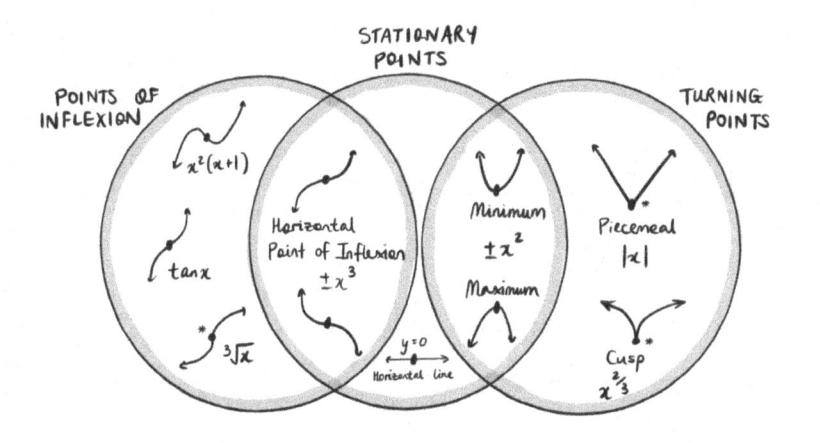

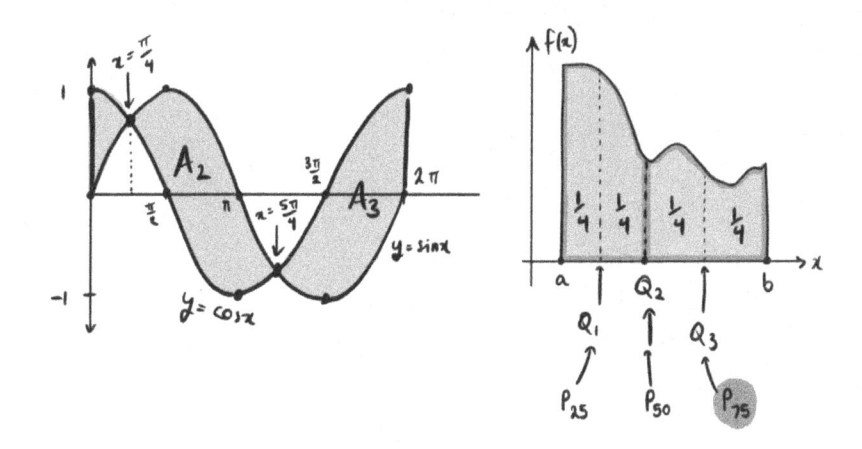

POINTS OF INFLEXION

- $x^2(x+1)$
- $\tan x$
- $\sqrt[3]{x}$

STATIONARY POINTS

- Horizontal Point of Inflexion $\pm x^3$
- $y=0$ Horizontal line
- Minimum $\pm x^2$
- Maximum

TURNING POINTS

- Piecemeal $|x|$
- Cusp $x^{\frac{2}{3}}$

Graph showing $y = \sin x$ and $y = \cos x$ with regions A_2, A_3, marked points at $x = \frac{\pi}{4}$, $\frac{\pi}{2}$, π, $x = \frac{5\pi}{4}$, $\frac{3\pi}{2}$, 2π.

Graph of $f(x)$ divided into four regions each of area $\frac{1}{4}$ between a and b, with quartiles Q_1, Q_2, Q_3 corresponding to percentiles P_{25}, P_{50}, P_{75}.

©2021 Eddie Woo

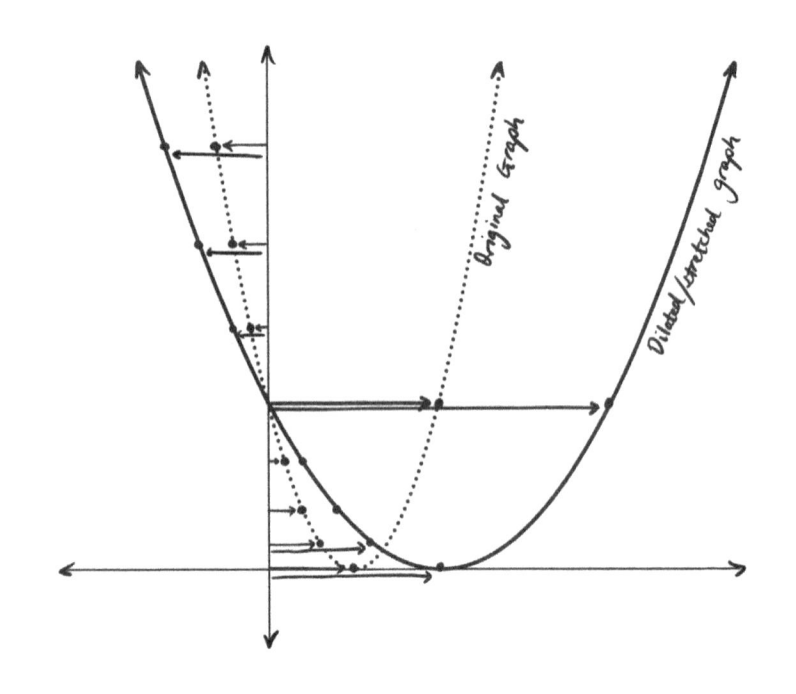

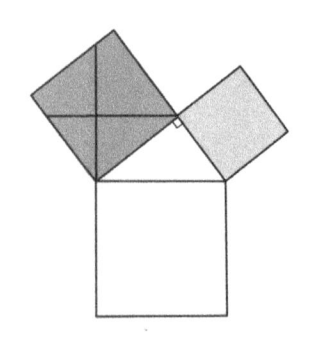

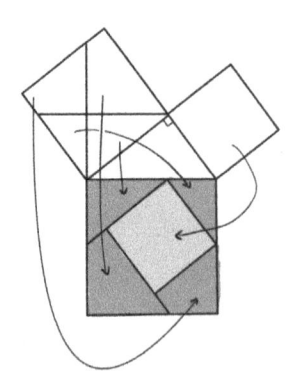

©2021 Eddie Woo

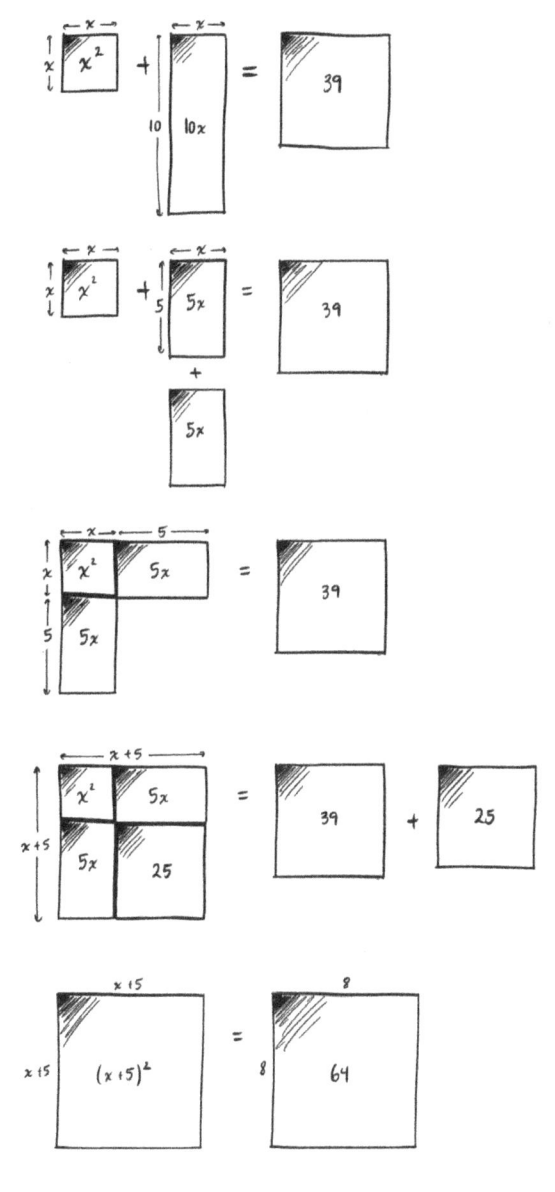

Eddie Woo's Resources for Students and Teachers

For Students

- *Eddie Woo's Magical Maths* and *Eddie Woo's Magical Maths 2* – fun mathematics activities for primary school students.
- *Woo's Wonderful World of Maths* – the surprising mathematics hidden all around us.
- *Wootube, www.youtube.com/misterwootube* – videos of live lessons straight from Eddie's classroom, uploaded every day.
- *Teenage Boss* on ABC iView, *https://iview.abc.net.au/show/teenage-boss* – a TV show all about learning the usefulness of maths in managing money.
- *Mathematics is the sense you never knew you had, https://www.youtube.com/watch?v=PXwStduNw14* – Eddie's TED talk all about mathematics.

For Teachers

- *Wootube^2, www.youtube.com/misterwootube2* – Eddie's YouTube channel for educators with ideas for classroom teaching and interviews about mathematics.
- Eddie's teacher resource website, *https://misterwootube.com/learning/worksheets/* – materials for learning and assessment in Years 7-12.

About Rebecca Lim

Rebecca Lim is a Melbourne writer, illustrator, editor and lawyer. She is the author of over twenty books, including *Tiger Daughter* and *The Children of the Dragon* series. Her work has been shortlisted for the Prime Minister's Literary Awards and Foreword INDIES Book of the Year Awards, shortlisted multiple times for the Aurealis Awards and Davitt Awards and longlisted for the Gold Inky Award and the David Gemmell Legend Award. Her novels have been translated into German, French, Turkish, Portuguese, Polish and Russian.

Like Eddie, Rebecca was a full-on English and English Literature geek in high school and loved Biology and Chemistry (although Maths was also not her thing, and she muddled through that, hoping for the best).

Rebecca was a migrant, just like Eddie's parents were and, when she was growing up, *never* saw any characters in children's books that looked like her, or like Eddie. Rebecca will never stop trying to ensure that Own Voice stories – just like Eddie's – are heard and read and widely shared.